P9-DWY-543

the**wines**of**italy**

The Quality of Life

BY **BURTON ANDERSON**

ITALY ON THE WEB

Visit WWW.ITALIANMADE.COM – a user friendly
website, exclusively dedicated to
the wines and food of Italy

An amazing wealth of information about Italian wines is offered
on www.italianmade.com, the most comprehensive database
for Italian wines (and foods) available. Here you will find a
clearly organized, in-depth discussion of every wine product in every
region of Italy, with full description of DOC appellations, invaluable
wine maps and accounts of varietals, producers, etc. The site will put
you in touch with the importers and distributors as well.

Not only does www.italianmade.com offer a description of any
bottle imported into the U.S., it also tells you about the foods of its
region and how and where they can be obtained, so that you can
offer your guests a "virtual visit " to any area of Italy. This marvelously
comprehensive website should be an invaluable source in planning
your wine list and a unique aid in menuing, food and wine pairing,
event planning, and many other means of offering guests the most
fulfilling Italian experience possible.

www.italianmade.com

Published by the Italian Trade Commission
Sponsored by the Italian Ministry of Agricultural, Food and Forestry Resources
© /t The Italian Trade Commission, New York, 2001
The text was written by Burton Anderson
6th Edition

Table of Contents

Introduction ⎯⎯⎯⎯⎯⎯⎯⎯ 5
Italian Wine Through the Ages ⎯⎯⎯⎯⎯ 7
Wine Laws & Labels ⎯⎯⎯⎯⎯⎯ 9
Glossary ⎯⎯⎯⎯⎯⎯⎯⎯⎯ 11
Map of DOC and DOCG Production Areas ⎯⎯ 15
A Review of Italian Wines ⎯⎯⎯⎯⎯ 16

The South and Islands: Oenotria Revisited ⎯⎯ 17
Sicily ⎯⎯⎯⎯⎯⎯⎯⎯⎯ 19
Sardinia ⎯⎯⎯⎯⎯⎯⎯⎯ 23
Calabria ⎯⎯⎯⎯⎯⎯⎯⎯ 26
Basilicata ⎯⎯⎯⎯⎯⎯⎯⎯ 29
Apulia ⎯⎯⎯⎯⎯⎯⎯⎯⎯ 31
Campania ⎯⎯⎯⎯⎯⎯⎯⎯ 34

Central Italy: Renaissance in the Heartland ⎯⎯ 37
Latium ⎯⎯⎯⎯⎯⎯⎯⎯⎯ 39
Molise ⎯⎯⎯⎯⎯⎯⎯⎯⎯ 42
Abruzzi ⎯⎯⎯⎯⎯⎯⎯⎯ 44
Marches ⎯⎯⎯⎯⎯⎯⎯⎯ 46
Umbria ⎯⎯⎯⎯⎯⎯⎯⎯⎯ 49
Tuscany ⎯⎯⎯⎯⎯⎯⎯⎯ 52

North by Northwest: From the Adriatic to Mont Blanc ⎯ 58
Emilia-Romagna ⎯⎯⎯⎯⎯⎯ 60
Liguria ⎯⎯⎯⎯⎯⎯⎯⎯⎯ 64
Lombardy ⎯⎯⎯⎯⎯⎯⎯⎯ 66
Piedmont ⎯⎯⎯⎯⎯⎯⎯⎯ 70
Valle d'Aosta ⎯⎯⎯⎯⎯⎯⎯ 75

The Northeast: Taste of the Future in the Venezie ⎯ 77
Veneto ⎯⎯⎯⎯⎯⎯⎯⎯⎯ 79
Friuli-Venezia Giulia ⎯⎯⎯⎯⎯⎯ 83
Trentino-Alto Adige ⎯⎯⎯⎯⎯⎯ 87

Italian Food and Wine ⎯⎯⎯⎯⎯⎯ 93
Index of DOC and DOCG wines ⎯⎯⎯⎯ 99
Other References on Italian Wines ⎯⎯⎯⎯ 104

An Invitation to an Adventure in Taste

Italy's glowing reputation with wine is due not only to the fact that it produces and exports more than any other country but that it offers the greatest variety of types, ranging through nearly every color, flavor and style imaginable.

Italian producers have moved rapidly to the forefront of world enology, improving techniques to create wines of undeniable class in every region, north and south. Their wines derive not only from native vines, which represent an enormous array, but also from a complete range of international varieties.

In the past it was sometimes said that Italians kept their best wines to themselves while supplying foreign markets with tasty but anonymous *vino* in economy sized bottles. But markets have changed radically in recent times as consumers in many lands—most importantly in Italy itself— have insisted on better quality.

For a while it may have seemed that the worldwide trend to standardize vines and wines was bound to compromise Italy's role as the champion of diversity. But, instead, leading producers in many parts of the country have kept the emphasis firmly on traditional vines. They have taken the authentic treasures of their ancient land and enhanced them in modern wines whose aromas and flavors are not to be experienced anywhere else. Getting to know the unique wines of Italy is an endless adventure in taste.

Experts increasingly rate Italy's premier wines among the world's finest. Many of the noblest originate in the more than 300 zones officially classified as DOC or DOCG—or, more recently, in areas recognized for typical wines under IGT (see Wine Laws & Labels). But a number of special wines carry their own proudly individualistic identities. Wine drinkers abroad, not always aware of the wealth of types (or perhaps overwhelmed by the numbers), have not always taken advantage of this unmatchable variety.

This booklet provides a basic reference to the wines of Italy through a survey of the 20 regions. It begins in the south, in those sunny Mediterranean places that the ancient Greeks came to call Oenotria, the land of wine, and moves north through the historic hills past Rome and Florence and over the Apennines to the Po valley and the Alps, with some of Europe's highest vineyards.

Vital if brief information is given on each region's geography and climate, production figures, grape varieties, traditions and trends, along with listings and abbreviated descriptions of DOC/DOCG and other important wines. There are also notes on Italy's wine laws and how to read a label, as well as a glossary of terms and references to books for deeper reading. This booklet is designed to be compact enough to carry around yet thorough enough to answer many of the questions that might arise while selecting, serving or tasting Italian wines.

A final feature discusses Italian food, *la cucina italiana*, which has become the preferred way of eating in much of the world today. From the vast array of regional dishes, a selection of specialties are suggested along with wines to drink with them.

Italian Wine through the Ages

taly's modern prodigiousness with wine scarcely begins to tell the story of its people's perennial links to the vine. The nature of the place—the influence of Mediterranean sunshine and mountain air currents on the hillsides of the elongated peninsula and islands—favors what seems to be an almost spontaneous culture of wine.

The heritage dates back some 4,000 years to when prehistoric peoples pressed wild grapes into juice that, as if by magic, fermented into wine. The ancient Greeks, expanding into Italy's southern reaches, dubbed the colonies Oenotria, the land of wine.

Etruscans were subtle and serene practitioners of the art of winemaking in the hills of central Italy, as attested by the art and artifacts left in their spacious tombs. The ancient Liguri produced and traded wine in northwestern Italy and southeastern France.

The Romans propagated the cult of Bacchus to all corners of the empire, developing a flourishing trade in wine throughout Mediterranean lands and beyond. So sophisticated was their knowledge of viticulture and enology that their techniques were not equaled again until the 17th or 18th centuries when Italians and other Europeans began to regard the making of wine as science rather than mystique.

Winemaking in Italy advanced rapidly through the 19th century, as methods of vinification and aging were improved and the use of corks to seal reinforced bottles and flasks permitted orderly shipping of wine worldwide. Such names as Chianti, Barolo and Marsala became known in Europe and beyond.

A century ago, several Italian wines were recognized as among the finest of their type: mainly Piedmontese and Tuscan reds from the Nebbiolo and Sangiovese varieties, but also white wines, still and sparkling, dry or sweet, merited international respect. Growers had complemented their local varieties with foreign vines, such as Cabernet, Merlot and the Pinots. There was evidence, then as now, that Italy's multifarious climates and terrains favored vines of many different types and styles, and consumers elsewhere in Europe and in North America had come to appreciate these new examples of class.

Then came phylloxera and other scourges to devastate Europe's vineyards around the turn of the century. Italian growers, who had been working with thousands of local varieties, were forced to reduce the numbers. Many opted for newly developed, more productive clones of both native and foreign vines. Taking advantage of the long, sunny growing season, they forced yields upward, reasoning that there was usually more profit to be made from quantity than quality.

Through the hard times of wars and depression, Italy

became one of the world's leading purveyors of low cost wine, often sold in containers of outlandish shapes and sizes. Though such practices were profitable for some, they did little for the image of Italian wine abroad.

For decades responsible producers had been trying to tighten regulations and put the emphasis on premium quality. But it was not until the denominazione d'origine laws were passed in the 1960s that a new climate of dignity and trust created the base for what came to be known as the modern renaissance of Italian wine.

Since Vernaccia di San Gimignano became the first DOC in 1966, the list has grown to include more than 300 zones delimited geographically, within which a multitude of wines are controlled for authenticity (see details under Wine Laws & Labels.) DOC/DOCG wines represent less than 20 percent of the total. Beyond them come a growing number of wines that qualify under the recently introduced category of indicazione geografica tipica (IGT). The "typical" category applies to wines that range from locally admired to internationally acclaimed.

Despite the reduction through this century, Italy still has more types of vines planted than any other country, including natives and a virtually complete range of the so-called international varieties. The number of officially approved Vitis vinifera varieties runs well into the hundreds, and there are even a few non-vinifera vines and hybrids used here and there by the nation's countless do-it-yourself winemakers.

This heritage of vines permits Italy to produce a greater range of distinctive wines than any other nation. Though Italy is most noted for its noble reds for aging, trends also favor more immediate types of rosso, including the vini novelli to be drunk within months of the harvest. Italy is also a major producer of white wines, ranging in style from light and fruity to oak-matured versions of impressive substance and depth. Some regions are noted for bubbly wines, whether the lightly fizzy frizzante or the fully sparkling spumante made by either the sealed tank charmat or bottle-fermented classico or tradizionale method.

This wealth of wines may seem overwhelming. Consumers outside Italy are sometimes bewildered by the assortment of names of places, grape varieties, proprietors and types and in exasperation turn to more comprehensible sources for wine.

This booklet is designed to provide readers with clear and concise information that should allay some of the confusion. But it cannot offer a shortcut to the mastery of Italian wines. That can come only through experience, as wine drinkers overcome taste prejudices and the fear of the unknown to appreciate why Italian winemakers are proud to be different in an age of uniformity.

Without staking claims to supremacy, it seems fair to submit that numerous Italian wines stand with the international elite. But what is perhaps most encouraging is that Italy's premium production continues to expand and improve. Italians have become increasingly committed to meeting the growing demand for wines of quality and character at every level of price.

Wine Laws & Labels

Italians over the centuries have pioneered laws to control the origins and protect the names of wines. The ancient Romans defined production areas for dozens of wines. In 1716, the Grand Duchy of Tuscany delimited the zones for important wines, setting a precedent for modern legislation.

Yet only since the mid-1960s have controls been applied nationwide under what is known as denominazione di origine controllata or, by the initials, as DOC. There are now more than 300 DOC appellations, all delimited geographically. Wines from 22 zones have been further distinguished as DOCG, the G for garantita or guaranteed authenticity of wines of "particular esteem." DOCG has expanded from the original five—Barbaresco, Barolo, Brunello di Montalcino, Vino Nobile di Montepulciano and Chianti—to cover 17 other zones around the country where wines must meet standards of typology and quality imposed by commissions of experts.

Within the DOC and DOCG zones well over 2,000 types of wine are produced. They may be defined by color or type (still, bubbly or sparkling; dry, semisweet or sweet; natural or fortified). Or they may be referred to by grape variety (e.g. Trentino has 26 types of wine including 20 varietals). Wines may also be categorized by age (young wine to be sold in the year of harvest as novello or aged as vecchio, stravecchio or riserva) or by a special subzone as classico or superiore. The term superiore or scelto may also apply to a higher degree of alcohol, a longer required period of aging or lower vine yields. (Most definitions can be found in the Glossary).

DOC applies to wines from specified grape varieties grown in delimited zones and vinified and aged following set methods to meet prescribed standards of color, odor, flavor, alcohol content, acidity, and so on. Regulations of each DOC are determined by producers in the zone (often grouped in a consortium) guided by the national wine committee.

DOC/DOCG zones may range in scale from the vineyard areas of an entire region down to a few choice plots around a remote village. DOC and DOCG wines rate the European Union designation VQPRD (for quality wine produced in determined regions).

Recent changes in the wine laws opened the way for DOC and DOCG wines to carry names of communities, areas of geographical or historical importance in the zones and names of individual vineyards of established reputation. Yet in recent times DOC and DOCG have accounted for only about 20 percent of Italy's production. The addition of the IGT (indicazione geografica tipica) system of recognizing "typical" wines is rapidly expanding the number of official appellations.

Curiously, up to now, some of Italy's finest wines have been referred to as vini da tavola, "table wines" made by producers who by chance or by choice worked outside the DOC norms. Most such wines now fall into IGT categories, such as Toscano in Tuscany or Sicilia in Sicily. Those wines must be made from approved grape varieties in blends or alone, in which case the varietal may be mentioned on labels.

The aim is to increase the proportion of classified wines to a majority of national production. But it is important to remember that the most reliable guide to the quality of any wine from anywhere is the reputation of the individual producer or estate. Certain names are worth getting to know.

Labels of DOC/DOCG and IGT wines must carry the official appellation, the producer's or bottler's name and commune of bottling, the quantity of wine contained (certified by the letter **e**); and the alcohol grade by volume. DOCG wines must have the official pink strip seal at the top of the bottle. Wines exported outside of the European Union must be certified by chemical analysis and labeled to meet standards of the importing nation. Wines shipped to North America carry the official red seal with the initials INE.

Glossary

The following Italian terms may be found on labels or literature about wine.

Abboccato - Lightly sweet.

Alcool - Alcohol, usually stated by % of volume.

Amabile – Semisweet.

Annata - Vintage year.

Azienda agricola or agraria or vitivinicola - Farm or estate which produces all or most of the grapes for wine sold under its labels.

Bianco - White.

Botte - Cask or barrel.

Bottiglia - Bottle.

Brut – Dry (sparkling wine).

Cantina - Cellar or winery.

Cantina sociale - Cooperative winery.

Casa vinicola - Wine house or merchant (commerciante) whose bottlings come mainly from purchased grapes or wines.

Cascina - Farmhouse, often used for estate.

Cerasuolo - Cherry-hued rosé.

Chiaretto - Deep rosé.

Classico - The historic core of a DOC zone.

Consorzio - Consortium of producers.

Dolce - Sweet.

Enoteca - Literally wine library, referring to both publicly sponsored displays and privately owned shops.

Enologo - Enologist with a university degree; enotecnico is a winemaking technician with a diploma.

Ettaro - Hectare (2.471 acres) the standard measure of vineyard surface in Italy

Ettolitro - Hectoliter, or 100 liters, the standard measure of wine volume in Italy

Etichetta - Label.

Fattoria - Farm or estate.

Frizzante or Frizzantino - Fizzy or faintly fizzy.

Imbottigliata - Bottled (all'origine implies at the source)

Invecchiato - Aged.

Liquoroso - Strong wine, sometimes fortified but usually of naturally high alcoholic grade.

Maso - A holding, often referring to a vineyard or estate.

Masseria - Farm or estate.

Metodo Charmat - Sparkling wine made by the sealed tank method.

Metodo classico or tradizionale - Terms for sparkling wine made by the bottle fermentation method, replacing the terms champenois or champenoise, which can no longer be used in Italy.

Millesimato – Vintage dated sparkling wine.

Passito or Passita - Partially dried grapes and the strong, usually sweet wines made from them.

Podere - Small farm or estate.

Produttore - Producer.

Recioto -Wine made from partly dried grapes, often sweet and strong.

Riserva - Reserve, for DOC or DOCG wine aged a specific time.

Rosato - Rosé.

Rosso - Red.

Scelto – Selected, term used for certain DOC wines. Auslese in German (Alto Adige).

Secco - Dry.

Semisecco - Medium sweet, usually in sparkling wine.

Spumante - Sparkling in dry or sweet wines

Superiore - Denotes DOC wine that meets standards above the norm (higher alcohol, longer aging, a special subzone), though conditions vary.

Tenuta - Farm or estate.

Uva - Grape.

Vecchio - Old, to describe aged DOC wines; Stravecchio, very old, applies to the longest aged Marsala and to some spirits.

Vendemmia - Harvest or vintage. Vendemmia tardiva or late harvest defines wines from grapes left to ripen fully on the vine

Vigna or vigneto - Vineyard. Vigna may be used under DOC/DOCG for approved single vineyard wines.

Vignaiolo/Viticoltore - Terms for grape grower.

Vino da tavola - Table wine, applies loosely to most non-DOCs.

Vino novello - New wine, usually red, that must be bottled and sold within the year of harvest.

Vitigno - Vine or grape variety.

Vivace - Lively, as in lightly bubbly wines.

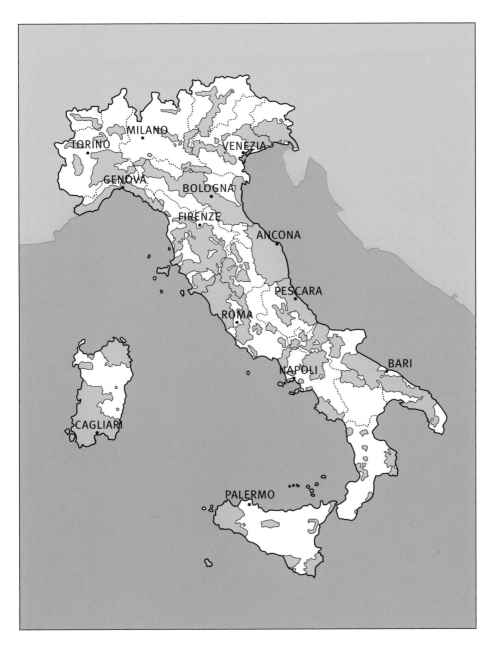

A Review of Italian Wines

The following survey of the wines of Italy's 20 regions follows a geographical pattern which divides the country into four sections: The South and Islands; Central regions; North Central and Northwest regions; Northeast regions. Similarities often exist within these sections in terms of climate and geography, as well as in grape varieties, vineyard maintenance and enological practices. But the divisions are rather arbitrary, designed more to aid the reader's orientation than to point up clear distinctions. Italian wines are most accurately perceived region by region.

Each of the 20 regions is a political entity with certain powers of its own in balance with national laws. Every region is further divided into provinces which take the name of a principal city or town. A capsule introduction to each region lists the capital and provinces, size and population, vineyard area and wine production and rank in each category. There is also a listing, first of DOC or DOCG wines and then of IGT wines. Since a great deal of information needed to be packed into limited space, each wine is described through abbreviations which follow this key:

R – Red (rosso)

W – White (bianco)

P – Pink (rosato, rosé, chiaretto, cerasuolo)

Dr – Dry (secco, brut)

Sw – Sweet or semisweet (dolce, amabile, abboccato)

Sp – Sparkling (spumante)

Fz – Fizzy or faintly bubbly (frizzante, frizzantino, vivace)

Ft – Fortified or naturally high in alcohol (liquoroso)

Rs – Reserve (riserva)

Sup – Superior (superiore, in reference to higher alcohol, longer aging or a specific subzone)

Ag – Aged, as required by DOC or DOCG in number of years

The South & Islands: Oenotria Revisited

Sicily, Sardinia, Calabria, Basilicata, Apulia, Campania

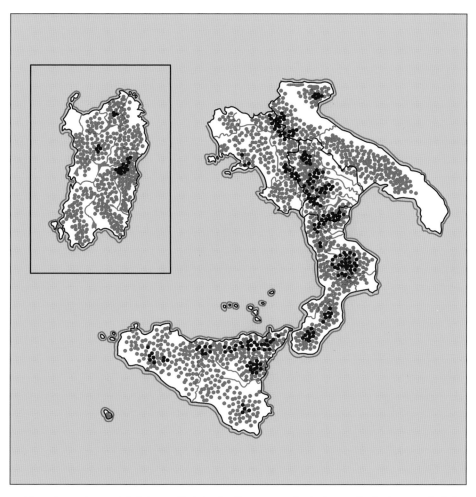

The six regions of Italy's south take in the sunwashed vineyards that prompted the ancient Greeks to nickname their colonies Oenotria, the land of wine. From Hellas they brought to Magna Græcia vines which are still planted today, under such names as Aglianico, Greco, Malvasia, Gaglioppo and Moscato.

The Romans in their turn recognized the potential of the slopes that gave them Falernum, Caecubum, Mamertinum and other heady wines that were eulogized by poets from Horace to Virgil. Pliny the Elder and Columella were among those who recorded methods of viticulture and enology that included descriptions of how to age and preserve wine and even to make it bubbly. But wine had its ups and downs under the Romans, too, reaching a low point when the Emperor Domitian ordered vines removed while restricting trade to combat excess production.

Many outsiders left their marks on these Mediterranean shores. Foremost among them were the Spaniards, who dominated until the Risorgimento and brought vines into Sardinia, Sicily and other places centuries after the Arabs and Phoenicians planted what may have been the first "foreign" vines in Italy.

It might be argued that at times in the past the vineyards of the Italian Mezzogiorno were put to better use than they had been until just recently. Apulia and Sicily have been perennial leaders in volume produced, much of it in bulk blending wines shipped to northerly places. Though the six regions produce nearly 40 percent of Italy's total wine, they account for only about 14 percent of the DOC/DOCG. Yet, after decades in which the emphasis had been steadfastly on quantity, producers in all regions have become increasingly convinced that the future lies in quality, as the class of wines steadily improves while volume steadily decreases.

Studied techniques of grape growing and methods of temperature controlled fermentation and maturation in oxygen-free conditions have permitted production of dry, balanced wines that can be attractively light and fruity. Several of Italy's most impressive red wines for aging originate in the south, led by Campania's DOCG of Taurasi. White wines of modern style have also come forth. There has been a welcome trend to upgrade the quality and status of the traditional sweet wines, such as Moscato and Malvasia, as well as Sicily's fortified Marsala and Sardinia's Vernaccia di Oristano.

The misconception that the Mezzogiorno has a universally torrid climate overlooks the fact that much of the territory is temperate and parts are downright chilly. Conditions depend on altitude and proximity to the Tyrrhenian, Ionian or Adriatic seas. Some good wines are made in hot places—the slopes of Vesuvius, the isle of Ischia, Apulia's Salento peninsula, Sicily's western coast and Sardinia's Campidano. But many wines of scope come from higher, cooler places—the hills around Avellino in Campania, Basilicata's Vulture, Sicily's Etna and central highlands, Apulia's interior plateau and Sardinia's eastern coastal range.

Major wineries from elsewhere in Italy have been investing in the south, where the climate permits consistent quality from year to year to offer wines of premium class at reasonable prices.

Contrasts are not the least of those things in which Sicily abounds. So perhaps it is not surprising that this ancient island boasts one of Italy's most progressive wine industries or that a region noted chiefly in the past for strong and often sweet amber Marsala and Moscato has switched the emphasis toward lighter, fruitier wines—mainly white but also red.

Sicily, the largest island in the Mediterranean, has more vineyards than any other Italian region. Yet, with the emphasis shifting from quantity to quality, wine production has diminished recently to slightly less than that of Veneto.

A major share of the DOC is represented by Marsala, a wine originated by English merchant traders two centuries ago. Marsala remains Sicily's proudest wine despite the not so distant era of degradation when it was used mainly for cooking or flavored with various syrups and sweeteners. Recently it has enjoyed a comeback among connoisseurs, who favor the dry Marsala Vergine and Superiore Riserva with the warmly complex flavors that rank them with the finest fortified wines of Europe.

The only other DOC wine made in significant quantity in Sicily is the pale white, bone dry Bianco d'Alcamo, which is now part of the broader Alcamo appellation. Moscato di Pantelleria, from the remote isle off the coast of Tunisia, is among the richest and most esteemed of Italian sweet wines in the Naturale and Passito Extra versions. Malvasia delle Lipari, from the volcanic Aeolian isles, is a dessert wine as exquisite as it is rare.

The dry white and red wines of Etna, whose vines adorn the lower slopes of the volcano, can show class, as can the pale red but potent Cerasuolo di Vittoria. Production of the other traditional DOCs—the dry, red Faro and the sweet Moscatos of Noto and Siracusa—has been minimal in recent times. But the volume of premium wine is certain to increase with the additions to the DOC list of Contessa Entellina, Eloro, Menfi, Sciacca, Sambuca di Sicilia, Contea di Sclafani and Santa Margherita Belice.

Wines from several admired producers of Sicily have not been qualified as DOC, though most are now covered by the IGT of Sicilia or other appellations. Plans have been advanced to introduce a regionwide Sicilia DOC.

About 75 percent of Sicily's wine is produced by cooperatives, though a growing number of privately owned estates has put the emphasis on premium quality. Methods of vine training in the sunny, temperate hills have been changed to reduce yields of grapes for wines of real

Palermo is the administrative center of Sicily, whose other provinces include Agrigento, Caltanissetta, Catania, Enna, Messina, Ragusa, Siracusa and Trapani. The largest of Italy's 20 regions (25,710 square kilometers), Sicily ranks 4th in population (5,098,000).

Vineyards cover 140,000 hectares, of which registered DOC plots total about 23,000 hectares.

Annual wine production of 8,100,000 hectoliters (2nd) includes about 3% DOC, of which more than 90% is white.

character and individuality. Recently, prominent wine houses from northern and central Italy have invested in vineyards on the island.

Such international varieties as Chardonnay, Sauvignon Blanc, Cabernet Sauvignon and the Pinots show real promise in Sicily. But some of the island's finest wines come from native varieties, notably Nero d'Avola (or Calabrese), Nerello Mascalese and Perricone (or Pignatello) among the reds and Inzolia and Grecanico among the whites. Sicily has taken the lead in winemaking in the modern south as producers seem increasingly determined to live up to the promise that was already admired millennia ago by the Greeks and Romans.

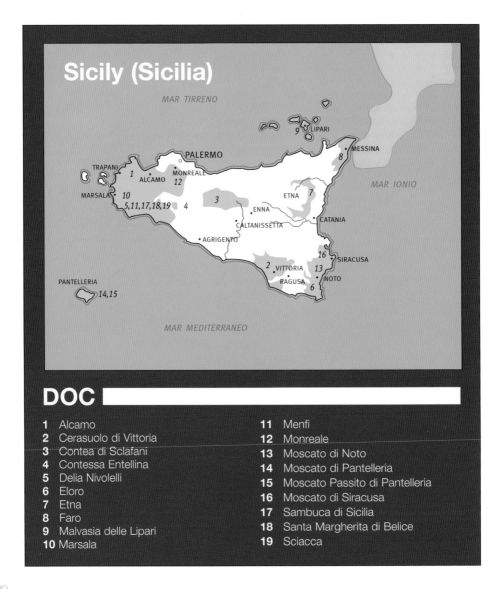

DOC

1	Alcamo	11	Menfi
2	Cerasuolo di Vittoria	12	Monreale
3	Contea di Sclafani	13	Moscato di Noto
4	Contessa Entellina	14	Moscato di Pantelleria
5	Delia Nivolelli	15	Moscato Passito di Pantelleria
6	Eloro	16	Moscato di Siracusa
7	Etna	17	Sambuca di Sicilia
8	Faro	18	Santa Margherita di Belice
9	Malvasia delle Lipari	19	Sciacca
10	Marsala		

Alcamo : Bianco di Alcamo W-Dr/Sp; Bianco Classico W-Dr; Rosato P-Dr/Sp; Rosso R-Dr, Rs Ag-2; Rosso Novello R-Dr; Vendemmia Tardiva W-Sw; Ansonica W-Dr; Cabernet Sauvignon R-Dr; Calabrese R-Dr; Catarratto W-DR; Chardonnay W-Dr; Grecanico W-Dr; Grillo W-Dr; Merlot R-Dr; Müller Thurgau W-Dr; Sauvignon W-Dr; Syrah R-Dr

Cerasuolo di Vittoria : R-Dr

Contea di Sclafani : Bianco W-Dr/Sp; Dolce W-Sw; Dolce Vendemmia Tardiva W-Sw Ag-1.5; Novello R-Dr; Rosato P-Dr/Sp; Rosso R-Dr; Ansonica W-Dr/Sp; Cabernet Sauvignon R-Dr, Rs Ag-2; Calabrese R-Dr, Rs Ag-2; Catarratto W-Dr/Sp; Chardonnay W-Dr/Sp; Grecanico W-Dr/Sp; Grillo W-Dr/Sp; Merlot R-Dr, Rs Ag-2; Nerello Mascalese R-Dr; Perricone R-Dr, Rs Ag-2; Pinot Bianco W-Dr/Sp; Pinot Nero R-Dr, Rs Ag-2; Sangiovese R-Dr, Rs Ag-2; Sauvignon W-Dr/Sp; Syrah R-Dr, Rs Ag-2

Contessa Entellina : Bianco W-Dr; Rosato P-Dr; Rosso R-Dr, Rs Ag-2; Ansonica W-Dr, Ansonica Vendemmia Tardiva W-Sw; Cabernet Sauvignon R-Dr; Chardonnay W-Dr; Grecanico W-DR; Merlot R-Dr; Pinot Nero R-Dr; Sauvignon W-Dr

Delia Nivolelli : Bianco W-Dr/Sp; Rosso R-Dr, Rs Ag-2; Ansonica W-Dr/Sp; Cabernet R-Dr, Rs Ag-2; Chardonnay W-Dr/Sp; Damaschino W-Dr/Sp; Grecanico Dorato W-Dr/Sp; Grillo W-Dr/Sp; Merlot R-Dr, Rs Ag-2; Müller Thurgau W-Dr/Sp; Nero d'Avola R-Dr, Rs Ag-2; Perricone or Pignatello R-Dr, Rs Ag-2; Sangiovese R-Dr, Rs Ag-2; Sauvignon W-Dr/Sp; Syrah R-Dr, Rs Ag-2

Eloro : Rosato P-Dr; Rosso R-DR; Frappato R-Dr; Nero d'Avola R-Dr; Pachino R-Dr, Rs Ag-2; Pignatello R-Dr

Etna : Bianco W-Dr; Bianco Sup W-Dr; Rosato P-Dr; Rosso R-Dr

Faro : R-Dr, Ag-1

Malvasia delle Lipari : W-Sw; Passito (also Dolce Naturale) W-Sw; Liquoroso W-Sw-Ft

Marsala : Oro or Ambro W-Dr/Sw/Ft; Rubino R-Dr/Sw/Ft; Fine Ag-1 (Oro, Ambro, Rubino, Secco, Semisecco, Dolce); Superiore Ag-2 (Oro, Ambro, Rubino, Secco, Semisecco, Dolce); Superiore Riserva Ag-4; Vergine or Soleras Ag-5 (Oro, Ambro, Rubino, Secco, Semisecco, Dolce); Ag-5, Vergine or Soleras Stravecchio or Riserva Ag-10; Cremovo or Cremovo Zabaione W-Sw or R-Sw

Menfi : Bianco W-Dr; Feudi dei Fiori W-Dr; Rosso R-Dr, Rs Ag-2; Vendemmia Tardiva W-Sw; Ansonica or Inzolia W-Dr; Bonera R-Dr Ag-1, Rs Ag-2; Cabernet Sauvignon R-Dr; Chardonnay W-Dr; Grecanico W-Dr; Merlot R-Dr; Nero d'Avola R-Dr; Sangiovese R-Dr

Monreale : Bianco W-Dr, also Sup; Novello R-Dr; Rosato P-Dr; Rosso R-Dr, Rs Ag-2; Ansonica or Inzolia W-Dr; Cabernet Sauvignon R-Dr, Rs Ag-2; Calabrese or Nero d'Avola R-Dr, Rs Ag-2; Catarratto W-Dr; Chardonnay W-Dr; Grillo W-Dr; Merlot R-Dr, Rs Ag-2; Perricone R-Dr, Rs Ag-2; Pinot Bianco W-Dr; Pinot Nero R-Dr, Rs Ag-2; Sangiovese R-Dr, Rs Ag-2; Syrah R-Dr, Rs Ag-2

Moscato di Noto : W-Sw; Spumante W-Sw-Sp; Liquoroso W-Sw-Ft

Moscato di Pantelleria : Naturalmente Dolce W-Sw; Spumante W-Sw-Sp; Liquoroso W-Sw-Ft

Moscato Passito di Pantelleria : W-Sw; Liquoroso W-Sw-Ft, Extra W-Sw Ag-1

Moscato di Siracusa : W-Sw

Sambuca di Sicilia : Bianco W-Dr; Rosato P-Dr; Rosso R-Dr, Rs Ag-2; Cabernet Sauvignon R-Dr; Chardonnay W-Dr

Santa Margherita di Belice : Bianco W-Dr; Rosso R-Dr; Ansonica W-Dr; Catarratto W-Dr; Grecanico W-Dr; Nero d'Avola R-Dr; Sangiovese R-Dr

Sciacca : Bianco W-Dr; Rosato P-Dr; Rosso R-Dr, Rs Ag-2; Riserva Rayana W-Dr, Rs Ag-2; Cabernet R-Dr; Chardonnay W-Dr; Grecanico W-Dr; Inzolia W-Dr; Merlot R-Dr; Nero d'Avola R-Dr; Perricone or Pignatello R-Dr, Rs; Sangiovese R-Dr

IGT (6)

Colli Ericini
Fontanarossa di Cerda
Salemi
Salina
Sicilia
Valle Belice

Sardinia (Sardegna)

Isolation in mid-Mediterranean has made Sardinia the most idiosyncratic of Italian regions. The island's history has been influenced as much by foreigners—Spaniards in particular—as by other Italians.

The island's vines tell a story of their own, frequently with a Spanish accent. The Mediterranean stalwarts are there in the various clones of Moscato and Malvasia, but several other varieties are unique in Italy, such as Girò, Cannonau, Nuragus, Monica, Semidano, Torbato and Vernaccia di Oristano.

Sardinians have sharply reduced vineyards and volume of production recently while notably improving the general quality of wines. Among DOC wines, whites prevail by nearly two to one over reds.

The island's most productive vineyard area is the Campidano, the fertile plains and low rolling hills northwest of the capital and major port of Cagliari. The varieties grown there—Girò, Malvasia, Monica, Moscato, Nasco and Nuragus—carry the name of Cagliari in their denominations.

The wooded slopes of the northern Gallura peninsula and the northwestern coastal area around Sassari and Alghero are noted for premium whites. Vermentino dominates the dry wines, notably in Vermentino di Gallura DOCG, though the Torbato under Alghero DOC can be equally distinguished. Vermentino, a variety also planted in Liguria and parts of Tuscany, makes a white of winning style in the Gallura hills, though it can be produced throughout the region under the Sardinia DOC.

Moscato can be either still or sparkling, but it is always sweet, notably from Sorso and Sennori and the Gallura hills and the town of Tempio Pausania in the north. Malvasia may be sweet, but is perhaps most impressive dry from the town of Bosa and the Planargia hills on the western side of the island, as well as under the Cagliari DOC. Still another refined sweet white is Semidano, which has a DOC for all of Sardinia, though it is most noted from the town of Mogoro.

The most individual of Sardinian wines is Vernaccia di Oristano. From a vine of uncertain origin grown in the flat, sandy Tirso river basin around Oristano, it becomes a Sherry-like amber wine with a rich array of nuances in bouquet and flavor.

The most popular white variety is Nuragus, which is believed to have been brought there by the Phoenicians. Its name derives from the island's prehistoric stone towers known as nuraghe. Nuragus is the source of a modern dry white, clean and crisp, if rather bland in flavor.

Cagliari is the administrative center of Sardinia, whose other provinces include Nuoro, Oristano and Sassari. The region ranks 3rd in size (24,090 square kilometers) and 12th in population (1,654,000).

Vineyards cover 43,330 hectares, of which registered DOC or DOCG plots total 7,300 hectares.

Average annual wine production of 1,190,000 hectoliters (13th) includes more than 10% DOC or DOCG, of which about 60% is white.

DOCG

1 Vermentino di Gallura

DOC

2 Alghero
3 Arborea
4 Campidano di Terralba
5 Cannonau di Sardegna (Capo Ferrato, Jerzu, Oliena)*
6 Carignano del Sulcis
7 Girò di Cagliari
8 Malvasia di Bosa
9 Malvasia di Cagliari
10 Mandrolisai
11 Monica di Cagliari
12 Monica di Sardegna*
13 Moscato di Cagliari
14 Moscato di Sardegna (Gallura, Tempio Pausania)*
15 Moscato di Sorso Sennori
16 Nasco di Cagliari
17 Nuragus di Cagliari
18 Sardegna Semidano (Mogoro)*
19 Vermentino di Sardegna*
20 Vernaccia di Oristano

*Wines may be produced throughout the region

Sardinia (Sardegna)

The island's important red varieties are Cannonau, a relative of the Granacha brought from Spain, and Carignano and Monica, also of Spanish origin. Cannonau and Monica can be dry or sweet, though trends favor the dry type toned down in strength from its traditionally heroic proportions. Vineyards in the rugged eastern coastal range around Nuoro are noted for rich, red Cannonau. Wines of note comes from the towns of Oliena, Jerzu and Dorgali and the coastal hills of Capo Ferrato. Cannonau also makes a fine sweet wine, which can be reminiscent of Port.

A rising star among red wines is Carignano del Sulcis, from the southwest, where certain wineries have emerged with notable style recently. A curiosity among the reds is the moderately sweet Girò di Cagliari.

In addition to its 20 wines of DOC and DOCG, Sardinia has 16 IGTs, the most of any region.

DOCG (1)

Vermentino di Gallura : W-Dr, also Sup

DOC (19)

Alghero : Bianco W-Dr/Fz; Rosato P-Dr/Fz; Rosso R-Dr, also Novello; Liquoroso R-Sw-Ft, Ag-3, Rs Ag-5; Passito R-Sw or W-Sw; Spumante Bianco W-Dr-Sp; Spumante Rosso R-Dr-Sp; Cabernet R-Dr; Cagnulari R-Dr; Chardonnay W-Dr/Sp; Sangiovese R-Dr; Sauvignon W-Dr; Torbato W-Dr/Sp; Vermentino W-Dr/Fz

Arborea : Sangiovese R-P-Dr; Trebbiano W-Dr/Fz

Campidano di Terralba : R-Dr

Cannonau di Sardegna (Capo Ferrato, Jerzu, Oliena or Nepente di Oliena) : Rosato P-Dr; Rosso R-Dr, Rs Ag-2; Liquoroso Dolce Naturale R-Sw; Liquoroso Secco R-Dr-Ft

Carignano del Sulcis : R-Dr, Rs Ag-2, Sup Ag-2, Novello R-Dr, Passito R-Sw; Rosato P-Dr/Fz

Girò di Cagliari : Secco R-Dr; Liquoroso R-Sw-Ft, Rs Ag-2; Liquoroso Secco R-Dr-Ft, Rs Ag-2

Malvasia di Bosa : Dolce Naturale W-Sw Ag-2; Secco W-Dr Ag-2; Liquoroso Dolce W-Sw-Ft Ag-2; Liquoroso Secco W-Sw-Ft Ag-2

Malvasia di Cagliari : Secco W-Dr; Liquoroso W-Sw-Ft, Rs Ag-2; Liquoroso Secco W-Dr-Ft, Rs Ag-2

Mandrolisai : Rosato P-Dr; Rosso R-Dr, Sup Ag-2

Monica di Cagliari : Secco R-Dr; Liquoroso Dolce R-Sw-Ft, Rs Ag-2; Liquoroso Secco R-Sw-Ft, Rx Ag-2

Monica di Sardegna : R-Dr/Fz, Sup Ag-1

Moscato di Cagliari : W-Sw; Liquoroso W-Sw-Ft, Rs Ag-1

Moscato di Sardegna (Gallura, Tempio Pausania) : W-Sw/Sp

Moscato di Sorso Sennori : W-Sw; Liquoroso Dolce W-Sw-Ft

Nasco di Cagliari : Secco W-Dr; Liquoroso Dolce W-Sw-Ft, Rs Ag-2; Liquoroso Secco W-Dr-Ft, Rs Ag-2

Nuragus di Cagliari : W-Dr/Sw/Fz

Sardegna Semidano (Mogoro) : W-Sw/Sp; Passito W-Sw

Vermentino di Sardegna : W-Dr/Sw/Sp

Vernaccia di Oristano : W-Dr, Ag-2.5, Sup Ag-3.5; Liquoroso W-Sw-Ft Ag-2.5; Liquoroso Secco W-Dr-Ft Ag-2.5

IGT (16)

Barbagia
Camarro
Colli del Limbara
Isola dei Nuraghi
Marmilla
Nurra
Ogliastra
Parteolla
Planargia
Nuoro or Provincia di Nuoro
Romangia
Sibiola
Tharros
Trexenta
Valle del Tirso
Valli di Porto Pino.

Calabria

Catanzaro is the administrative center of Calabria, whose other provinces include Cosenza, Crotone, Reggio di Calabria and Vibo Valentia. The region ranks 10th in both size (15,080 square kilometers) and population (2,064,000).

Vineyards cover 31,600 hectares, of which registered DOC plots total 3,600 hectares.

Average annual wine production of 800,000 hectoliters (16th), includes 4.4% DOC, of which about 90% is red.

Calabria, which forms the toe of the Italian boot, is a predominately mountainous region with marked variations in microclimates between the sunny coastal hills along the Ionian and Tyrrhenian seas and the chilly heights of the Sila and Aspromonte massifs. Two grape varieties of Greek origin dominate—Gaglioppo in red wines, Greco in whites—though the types of wine they make can vary markedly from one place to another.

Calabria's best-known wine is Cirò, which grows in low hills along the Ionian coast between the ancient Greek cities of Sybaris and Kroton (Sibari and Crotone today). Local legend has it that Cirò descended directly from Krimisa, the wine Calabrian athletes drank to celebrate victory in an early Olympiad.

Lately Cirò has taken on contemporary touches as new methods of vine training and temperature-controlled winemaking have diminished the alcoholic strength (as well as the propensity to oxidize), making the wine rounder, fuller in fruit and fresher in bouquet. The classic Cirò is red, which in the reserve version has the capacity to age beyond a decade from certain vintages. There is also a rosato to drink young and a bianco from Greco grapes that can show impressive youthful freshness.

Melissa, an adjacent DOC zone, makes red and white wines similar to Cirò. But red wines from the same Gaglioppo grown at higher altitudes—Pollino, Donnici and Savuto, for example—are lighter in body and color, sometimes with fresh scents and flavors reminiscent of Alpine reds. The dark Greco Nero variety is also used in certain reds of Calabria.

Recent experiments have also shown unexpected class in the ancient Magliocco variety for red wines, as well as convincing style with Cabernet Sauvignon. Chardonnay and Sauvignon also show promise in Calabria's hills.

Among the whites, the rare Greco di Bianco stands out as an exquisite but increasingly rare sweet wine. From a local variety of Greco grown near the Ionian coast at the town of Bianco, it has a rich, velvety texture and an intriguing citrus-like bouquet. The nearly identical Greco di Gerace is a non-DOC wine that carries the ancient place name. From the same area comes Mantonico di Bianco, a Sherry-like amber wine with hints of almond and citrus in bouquet and flavor.

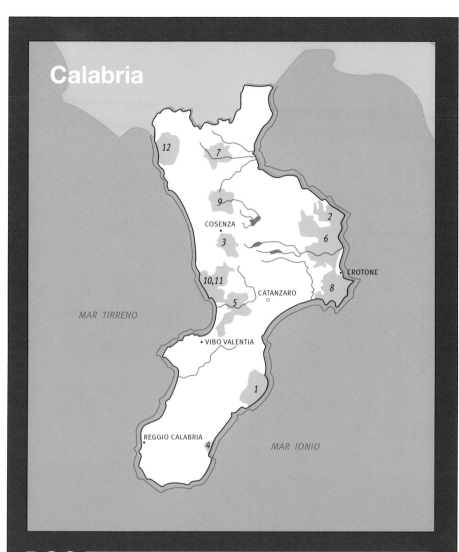

Calabria

COSENZA

CROTONE

CATANZARO

MAR TIRRENO

VIBO VALENTIA

REGGIO CALABRIA

MAR IONIO

DOC

1 Bivongi
2 Cirò
3 Donnici
4 Greco di Bianco
5 Lamezia
6 Melissa

7 Pollino
8 Sant'Anna di Isola Capo Rizzuto
9 San Vito di Luzzi
10 Savuto
11 Scavigna
12 Verbicaro

DOC (12)

Bivongi : Bianco W-Dr; Rosato P-Dr; Rosso R-Dr, Rs Ag-2, also Novello R-Dr

Cirò : Bianco W-Dr; Rosato P-Dr; Rosso R-Dr, also Classico and Sup, Rs Ag-2

Donnici : Bianco W-Dr; Rosato P-Dr; Rosso R-Dr, Rs Ag-2, also Novello R-Dr

Greco di Bianco : W-Sw Ag-1

Lamezia : Bianco W-Dr; Rosato P-Dr; Rosso R-Dr, Rs Ag-3, also Novello R-Dr; Greco W-Dr

Melissa : Bianco W-Dr; Rosso R-Dr, Sup Ag-2

Pollino : R-Dr, Sup Ag-2

Sant'Anna di Isola Capo Rizzuto : R-Dr

San Vito di Luzzi : Bianco W-Dr; Rosato P-Dr; Rosso R-Dr

Savuto : R-Dr, Sup Ag-2

Scavigna : Bianco W-Dr; Rosato P-Dr; Rosso R-Dr

Verbicaro : Bianco W-Dr; Rosato P-Dr; Rosso R-Dr, Rs Ag-3

IGT (13)

Arghillà
Calabria
Condoleo
Costa Viola
Esaro
Lipuda
Locride
Palizzi
Pellaro
Scilla
Val di Neto
Valdamato
Valle del Crati.

Basilicata, also known as Lucania, is an often neglected region of arid hills and desolate mountains that can be bitterly cold for a southerly place. But the cool upland climate has its advantages for viticulture, in wines that can show enviable aromas and flavors.

Basilicata has only one DOC in Aglianico del Vulture, but that, at least, gives the inhabitants a source of pride. One of southern Italy's finest red wines, it is gradually gaining admirers elsewhere.

The Aglianico vine—which is also the base of Campania's vaunted Taurasi—was brought to Basilicata by the Greeks, perhaps as long ago as the 6th or 7th century BC. (Its name is a corruption of Hellenico). On the slopes of the extinct volcano known as Monte Vulture it makes a robust, deeply colored wine that from fine vintages can improve for many years, becoming increasingly refined and complex in flavor. There are also youthful versions of the wine, sometimes semisweet and even sparkling, but the dry vecchio or riserva, after aging in oak casks, rates the most serious consideration.

Aglianico is also used for wines under the region's single IGT of Basilicata, notably in the east around Matera, where reds from Sangiovese and Montepulciano also originate. White wines of interest are the sweet Moscato and Malvasia, the best of which come from the Vulture zone and the eastern Bradano valley.

Potenza is the administrative center of Basilicata, whose other province is Matera. The region ranks 14th in size (9,992 square kilometers) and 18th in population (608,000).

Vineyards cover 16,000 hectares, of which registered DOC plots total 1,450 hectares.

Average annual wine production of 550,000 hectoliters (17th) includes 2.2% DOC, entirely red.

DOC (1)

Aglianico del Vulture : R-Dr, Vecchio Ag-3, Rs Ag-5; Spumante R-Dr/Sw-Sp

IGT (1)

Basilicata

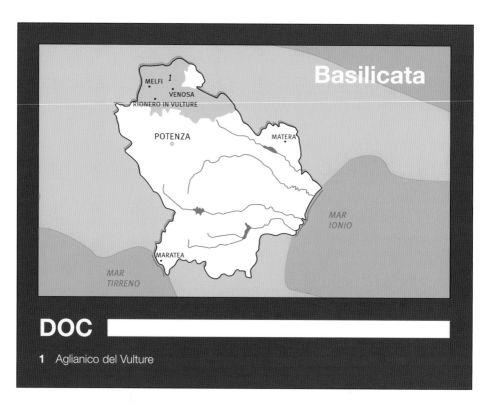

Basilicata

MELFI
1
VENOSA
RIONERO IN VULTURE

POTENZA

MATERA

MAR
IONIO

MARATEA

MAR
TIRRENO

DOC

1 Aglianico del Vulture

Apulia (Puglia)

Apulia, the heel of the Italian boot, is a long, relatively level region with a prolific production of wine. In the past, the region often surpassed Sicily and Veneto in output, though Apulia's former title of "Europe's wine cellar" no longer carries much weight.

As traditional markets for strong blending wines have diminished, Apulia's producers have increasingly put the accent on premium quality. Some have come forth with good to excellent wines: dry, balanced reds, whites and rosés, as well as sweet wines from a great range of grape varieties, both native and foreign.

Apulia has 25 DOC zones, the most of any southern region, yet, like its neighbors, it produces a small percentage of classified wine (just over 2%). Despite rapid improvement, Apulian wines have yet to establish a clear-cut reputation for excellence, though they are widely appreciated for value abroad.

Apulia can be divided roughly into two viticultural sectors by a hypothetical line crossing the region between Brindisi and Taranto. To the north, the terrain is rolling to hilly and the climate is temperate, even relatively cool at certain heights in the Murge plateau. Dry wines from there tend to have moderate strength, with impressive fruit, good acidity and ample bouquet.

Red wines generally derive from the native Uva di Troia or Bombino Nero, as well as Montepulciano and Sangiovese. White wines are dominated by the Verdeca variety, though Bianco d'Alessano, Malvasia, Trebbiano and Bombino Bianco are also evident.

The leading DOC zone of northern Apulia is Castel del Monte, the one appellation that enjoys an international reputation. It has a fine rosé and a full-bodied red that can be good young but often gains stature with age. In much of the north the emphasis is on red wines under such DOCs as Rosso Canosa, Rosso Barletta and Rosso di Cerignola.

Just north of the Brindisi-Taranto line white wines dominate, in particular those of the Itria valley—Locorotondo and Martina Franca—home of the conical roofed stone houses known as trulli. Throughout the region experimentation is under way with international varieties: Chardonnay, Pinot Bianco and Sauvignon among the whites; Cabernet, Merlot, Malbec and Pinot Nero among the reds.

South of the Brindisi-Taranto line lies Salento, a flat peninsula that extends between the Adriatic and Ionian seas to the easternmost point of Italy. Though hot, it is not quite torrid, thanks to the play of sea currents and the breezes that waft across the Adriatic from the Balkans.

Salento's traditional wines were the powerful, inky reds from

Bari is the administrative center of Apulia, whose other provinces include Brindisi, Foggia, Lecce and Taranto. The region ranks 7th in both size (19,363 square kilometers) and population (4,086,000).

Vineyards cover 132,000 hectares, of which registered DOC plots total 23,900 hectares.

Average annual wine production of 7,850,000 hectoliters (3rd) includes about 3.6% DOC, with somewhat more red than white.

Primitivo, Negroamaro and Malvasia Nera. But increasing attention is being given to fresher reds and rosés, as well as to some unexpectedly bright and fruity white wines.

Primitvo di Manduria, the early ripening variety of Salento is related to California's Zinfandel. Though it once served primarily as a blending wine, Primitivo from a new wave of producers has shown undeniable class in a style that stands comparison with its American counterparts.

Among the many DOCs of Salento, Salice Salentino stands out for its robust red and refined rosé, though wines from such appellations as Squinzano, Brindisi, Alezio and Copertino can show unexpected class. The Salento IGT applies to red wines that often carry individual names. White wines also show promise, Chardonnay in particular, though Salento is also renowned for flowery rosés that rank with Italy's finest.

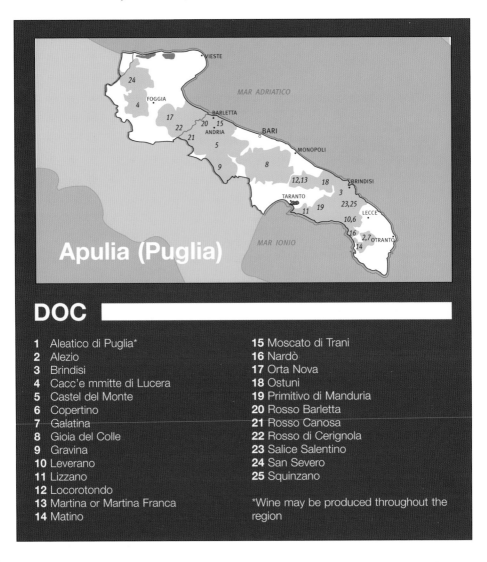

DOC

1 Aleatico di Puglia*	**15** Moscato di Trani
2 Alezio	**16** Nardò
3 Brindisi	**17** Orta Nova
4 Cacc'e mmitte di Lucera	**18** Ostuni
5 Castel del Monte	**19** Primitivo di Manduria
6 Copertino	**20** Rosso Barletta
7 Galatina	**21** Rosso Canosa
8 Gioia del Colle	**22** Rosso di Cerignola
9 Gravina	**23** Salice Salentino
10 Leverano	**24** San Severo
11 Lizzano	**25** Squinzano
12 Locorotondo	
13 Martina or Martina Franca	*Wine may be produced throughout the
14 Matino	region

DOC (25)

Aleatico di Puglia : Dolce Naturale R-Sw, Rs Ag-3; Liquoroso R-Sw-Ft, Rs Ag-3

Alezio : Rosato P-Dr; Rosso R-Dr, Rs Ag-2

Brindisi : Rosato P-Dr; Rosso R-Dr, Rs Ag-2

Cacc'e mmitte di Lucera : R-Dr

Castel del Monte : Bianco W-Dr/Fz; Rosato P-Dr/Fz; Rosso R-Dr, Rs Ag-2, also Novello; Aglianico R-Dr, Rs Ag-2; Aglianico Rosato P-Dr/Fz; Bombino Bianco W-Dr/Fz; Bombino Nero R-Dr; Cabernet R-Dr, Rs Ag-2; Chardonnay W-Dr/Fz; Pinot Bianco W-Dr/Fz; Pinot Nero R-Dr; Sauvignon W-Dr/Fz; Uva di Troia R-Dr, Rs Ag-2

Copertino : Rosato P-Dr; Rosso R-Dr, Rs Ag-2

Galatina : Bianco W-Dr/Fz; Rosato P-Dr/Fz; Rosso R-Dr, also Novello; Chardonnay W-Dr; Negroamaro R-Dr, Rs Ag-2

Gioia del Colle : Bianco W-Dr; Rosato P-Dr; Rosso R-Dr; Aleatico R-Sw, Rs Ag-2; Aleatico Liquoroso Dolce R-Sw; Primitivo R-Dr/Sw, Rs Ag-2

Gravina : W-Dr/Sw/Sp

Leverano : Bianco W-Dr; Bianco Passito W-Sw; Bianco Vendemmia Tardiva W-Dr/Sw; Rosato P-Dr; Rosso R-Dr, Rs Ag-2, also Novello; Malvasia Bianca W-Dr; Negroamaro Rosato P-Dr; Negroamaro Rosso R-Dr

Lizzano : Bianco W-Dr/Fz/Sp; Rosato P-Dr/Fz/Sp; Rosso R-Dr/Fz, also Novello; Malvasia Nera R-Dr, Sup Ag-1; Negroamaro Rosato P-Dr; Negroamaro Rosso R-Dr, Sup Ag-1

Locorotondo : W-Dr/Sp

Martina or Martina Franca : W-Dr/Sp

Matino : Rosato P-Dr; Rosso R-Dr

Moscato di Trani : Dolce Naturale W-Sw; Liquoroso W-Sw-Ft Ag-1

Nardò : Rosato P-Dr: Rosso R-Dr, Rs Ag-2

Orta Nova : Rosato P-Dr; Rosso R-Dr

Ostuni : Bianco W-Dr; Ottavianello R/P-Dr

Primitivo di Manduria : R-Dr; Dolce Naturale R-Sw; Liquoroso Dolce Naturale R-Sw Ag-2; Liquoroso Secco R-Dr Ag-2

Rosso Barletta : R-Dr, Invecchiato Ag-2

Rosso Canosa : R-Dr, Rs Ag-2; Canusium R-Dr, Rs Ag-2

Rosso di Cerignola : R-Dr, Rs Ag-2

Salice Salentino : Bianco W-Dr; Rosato P-Dr/Sp; Rosso R-Dr, Rs Ag-2; Aleatico Dolce R-Sw, Rs Ag-2; Aleatico Liquoroso Dolce R-Sw, Rs Ag-2; Pinot Bianco W-Dr/Sp

San Severo : Bianco W-Dr/Sp; Rosato P-Dr; Rosso R-Dr

Squinzano : Rosato P-Dr; Rosso R-Dr, Rs Ag-2

IGT (6)

Daunia
Murgia
Puglia
Salento
Tarantino
Valle d'Itria

Campania

Naples (Napoli) is the administrative center of Campania, whose other provinces include Avellino, Benevento, Caserta and Salerno. The region ranks 12th in size (13,595 square kilometers) and 2nd in population (5,793,000).

Vineyards cover 45,000 hectares, of which registered DOC or DOCG plots total 3,500 hectares.

Average annual wine production of 2,100,000 hectoliters (9th) includes about 5% DOC or DOCG, somewhat more white than red.

The ancient Romans admired Campania Felix as the most felicitous of wine regions. They favored the vineyards along the coast north of Naples where Falernian, the most treasured wine of the empire, was grown. They also praised the wines of volcanic Vesuvius and the wooded hills of Avellino. Even earlier, the Greeks had recognized the privileged nature of the place, introducing vines which still stand out today in Aglianico, Greco and Falanghina.

Yet, until recently, it seemed that wine producers of Campania, with a few conspicuous exceptions, had forgotten about the glories of the past, as growers left the land and winemakers largely ignored DOC. But now, after a long lapse, Campania is undergoing a revival that has dramatically improved quality.

Things truly are changing in Campania's vineyards, where a new spirit of achievement and sense of pride has been bolstered by the introduction of thoroughly modern winemaking techniques. Evidence of the new era is the rapid increase in production of DOC wines, including the first DOCG of the south in Taurasi. The volume of DOC wine produced has multiplied in recent years.

But modernization has by no means swept away respect for tradition. In Campania, a majority of producers strives to make the most of native vines, including an honor roll of so-called "archaeological varieties" which do indeed date back to antiquity.

The noblest of red varieties is Aglianico, which makes the red Taurasi, as well as the red Falerno del Massico and others. Taurasi has been called "the Barolo of the south," due to its size and ability to age, though its style is proudly its own.

Greco, a name applied to various vines prominent in the south, reaches heights in Greco di Tufo. Fiano, praised by the Romans, is the base of the inimitable Fiano di Avellino. Falanghina, which seems to have been the base of the white version of Falernian, has become the region's fastest spreading variety.

Campania's DOC zones also include the fabled islands of Capri and Ischia, as well as the recently revived Penisola Sorrentina and Costa d'Amalfi, taking in the dramatically terraced seaside vineyards from Sorrento to Amalfi.

DOCG (1)

Taurasi : R-Dr Ag-3, Rs Ag-4

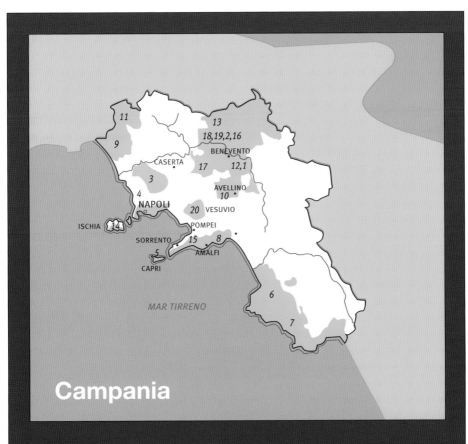

Campania

DOCG

1 Taurasi

DOC

2 Aglianico del Taburno
3 Aversa
4 Campi Flegrei
5 Capri
6 Castel San Lorenzo
7 Cilento
8 Costa d'Amalfi (Furore, Ravello, Tramonti)
9 Falerno del Massico

10 Fiano di Avellino
11 Galluccio
12 Greco di Tufo
13 Guardia Sanframondi o Guardiolo
14 Ischia
15 Penisola Sorrentina
16 Sannio
17 Sant'Agata de' Goti
18 Solopaca
19 Taburno
20 Vesuvio

(Nota a Giulio: Per tracciare i territori occupate delle zone DOC/DOCG di Campania bisogna riferirsi alla Carta Enografica Italiana di Civiltà del Bere)

DOC (19)

Aglianico del Taburno : Rosato P-Dr; Rosso R-Dr Ag-2, Rs Ag-3

Aversa : Asprinio W-Dr/Sp

Campi Flegrei : Bianco W-Dr; Rosso R-Dr, also Novello; Falanghina W-Dr/Sp; Piedirosso R-Dr, Rs Ag-2; Piedirosso Passito Dolce R-Sw; Piedirosso Passito Secco R-Dr

Capri : Bianco W-Dr; Rosso R-Dr

Castel San Lorenzo : Bianco W-Dr; Rosato P-Dr; Rosso R-Dr; Barbera R-Dr, Rs Ag-2; Moscato W-Sw/Sp; Moscato Lambiccato W-Sw

Cilento : Bianco W-Dr; Rosato P-Dr; Rosso R-Dr; Aglianico R-Dr Ag-1

Costa d'Amalfi (Furore, Ravello, Tramonti) : Bianco W-Dr; Rosato P-Dr; Rosso R-Dr, Rs Ag-2

Falerno del Massico : Bianco W-Dr; Rosso R-Dr Ag-1, Rs Ag-2; Primitivo R-Dr Ag-1, Rs Ag-2

Fiano di Avellino : W-Dr; Apianum W-Dr

Galluccio : Bianco W-Dr; Rosato P-Dr; Rosso R-Dr, Rs Ag-2

Greco di Tufo : W-Dr/Sp

Guardia Sanframondi or Guardiolo : Bianco W-Dr; Rosato P-Dr; Rosso R-Dr, Rs Ag-2, also Novello; Spumante W-Dr-Sp; Aglianico R-Dr, Rs Ag-2; Falanghina W-Dr

Ischia : Bianco W-Dr; Bianco Spumante W-Dr-Sp; Bianco Sup W-Dr; Rosso R-Dr; Biancolella W-Dr; Forastera W-Dr; Piedirosso or Per'e Palummo R-Dr; Piedirosso or Per'e Palummo Passito R-Sw

Penisola Sorrentina : Bianco W-Dr; Bianco Sorrento W-Dr; Rosso R-Dr/Fz; Rosso Sorrento R-Dr; Gragnano or Lettere R-Dr/Fz

Sannio : Bianco W-Dr/Fz; Rosato P-Dr/Fz; Rosso R-Dr/Fz, also Novello; Spumante Metodo Classico W-Dr-Sp Ag-1.2; Aglianico R-Dr/Sp, also Passito R-Sw; Rs Ag-2; Barbera R-Dr/Sp, also Passito R-Sw; Coda di Volpe W-Dr/Sp, also Passito W-Sw; Falanghina W-Dr/Sp, also Passito W-Sw; Fiano W-Dr/Sp; Greco W-Dr/Sp, also Passito W-Sw; Moscato W-Sw/Sp, also Passito W-Sw; Piedirosso R-Dr/Sp; Sciascinoso R-Dr/Sp, also Passito R-Sw

Sant'Agata de' Goti : Bianco W-Dr; Rosato P-Dr; Rosso R-Dr, also Novello; Aglianico R-Dr Ag-2, Rs Ag-3; Falanghina W-Dr, also Passito W-Sw; Greco W-Dr; Piedirosso R-Dr, Rs Ag-2

Solopaca : Bianco W-Dr; Rosato P-Dr; Rosso R-Dr, Sup Ag-1; Spumante W-Dr-Sp; Aglianico R-Dr Ag-1; Falanghina W-Dr

Taburno : Bianco W-Dr; Rosso R-Dr, also Novello; Spumante W-Dr-Sp; Coda di Volpe W-Dr; Falanghina W-Dr; Greco W-Dr; Piedirosso R-Dr

Vesuvio : Bianco W-Dr; Rosato P-Dr; Rosso R-Dr; Lacryma Christi W-P-R-Dr/Sp; Lacryma Christi Liquoroso W-Sw-Ft

IGT (9)

Beneventano
Colli di Salerno
Dugenta
Epomeo
Irpinia
Paestum
Pompeiano
Roccamonfina
Terre del Volturno

Central Italy: Renaissance in the Heartland

Latium, Molise, Abruzzi, Marches, Umbria, Tuscany

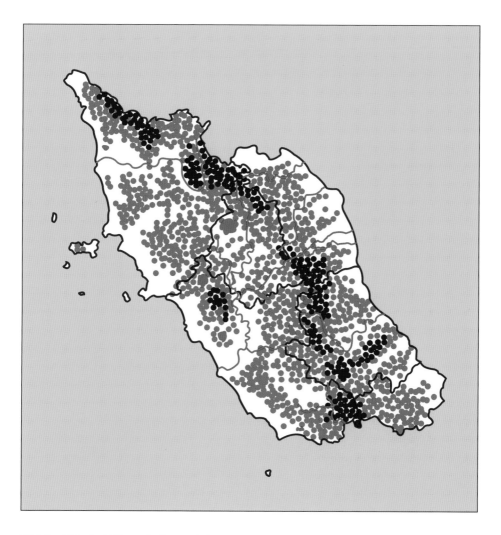

The historical hills at the heart of the peninsula, favored by ample sunshine and moderate temperatures, boast extensive natural conditions for fine wine. In the past, winemaking methods were often rustic. The practices of overproducing grapes and undervaluing scientific techniques sometimes squandered the excellent potential. But today the central regions, led by Tuscany with Chianti, Brunello and other noble reds, have moved to the forefront of Italian winemaking.

Between them, the six regions produce about 20 percent of the nation's wine and account for about 20 percent of the DOC or DOCG. The conflict between progress and tradition persists in places, but overall the renaissance in Italian wine has generated unrivaled momentum in the heartland. Still, there is no doubt that even greater things lie ahead.

The regions of central Italy are divided physically, and to some degree culturally, by the Apennines. To the west, on the Tyrrhenian side, lie Tuscany, Latium and landlocked Umbria. To the east, on the Adriatic side, lie Marches, Abruzzi and Molise. Viticulture on the Tyrrhenian side is dominated by the dark-skinned Sangiovese (whose various clones include some of Italy's noblest grapes for red wine) and the light-skinned Trebbiano and Malvasia (designed chiefly for quantities of tasty if rarely inspiring whites).

The realm of Sangiovese is Florence's region of Tuscany, where it prevails in Chianti—the nation's archetypal red—as well as in Brunello di Montalcino, Vino Nobile di Montepulciano and most of the noteworthy classified and many of the unclassified reds known as "Super Tuscans."

White Malvasia reigns in Rome's region of Latium. It is prominent in Frascati and the wines of the Alban hills, and combines with the ubiquitous Trebbiano in Est! Est!! Est!!! di Montefiascone and most other whites of the region. Umbrians have had the chance to pick and choose, favoring Sangiovese for their reds and the Procanico strain of Trebbiano for their prominent white Orvieto.

A trend, more evident in Tuscany than elsewhere, is to introduce noble outsiders— Cabernet Sauvignon, Merlot, the Pinots, Chardonnay and Sauvignon. But efforts are also being directed at upgrading such worthy natives as Vernaccia di San Gimignano, Umbria's Sagrantino and Grechetto and Latium's Cesanese.

The Adriatic regions have a rather neat and straight-forward structure of vines and wines. Vineyards are almost all planted in hills running in a tortuous strip between the sea and the mountains, where the climate is tempered by cool air currents.

Two native varieties stand out along the Adriatic coast, the white Verdicchio in the Marches and the red Montepulciano, which originated in the Abruzzi and is now widely planted elsewhere, including in Molise. The influences of Tuscany and Romagna can be tasted in Sangiovese (especially in the Marches) and Trebbiano (planted nearly everywhere that worthier varieties are not). Montepulciano can be remarkable on its own, though it also has a natural affinity for blends with Sangiovese in such fine reds as the Marches' Rosso Piceno and Rosso Conero.

Latium (Lazio)

Rome's region is intrinsically linked to white wine—to Frascati and Marino and the other golden-hued bianchi of the Castelli Romani, as well as to the fabled Est! Est!! Est!!! from the northern Latium town of Montefiascone.

The ancient Romans drank white wines, too, though Horace and company reserved their greatest praise for the red Falernian and Caecuban—which were grown along the coast in southern Latium and Campania. Although white wine accounts for an overwhelming share of the region's production, certain of its red wines seem more convincing to connoisseurs.

Latium's hills, favored by ample sunshine on fertile volcanic soils, seem to be naturally suited to the production of white wines based on various types of Malvasia and Trebbiano grapes. Rome's wines, led by Frascati and Marino, were traditionally abboccato, pleasingly soft though not so sweet as to overwhelm the flavor of food. They were easy, everyday wines not designed to last long or travel far.

The use of low temperature processing and sterile filtration have transformed their personalities into dryer, crisper, more durable wines with a propensity to travel that has opened up new commercial horizons. Still, with only occasional exceptions, the whites of Latium are pleasantly fleshy and fruity, wines that go enticingly well with a great range of foods but are not the sort to be laid away or fussed over.

Their immediacy is by no means a negative attribute, as evidenced by the established world market for Frascati, followed by Marino and less publicized but worthy neighbors such as Colli Albani, Colli Lanuvini, Castelli Romani, Velletri and Montecompatri Colonna. Though some admirers argue that the richer, stronger abboccato or cannellino versions are what Malvasia is all about, most modern consumers seem to prefer them softly dry.

Latium's DOC reds vary in composition. Aprilia, in the reclaimed stretches of what were once the Pontine Marshes, turns out considerable quantities of Merlot and Sangiovese. The reds of Cerveteri, Cori and Velletri are based on Montepulciano and Sangiovese. The native Cesanese makes richly flavored dry and sweet reds in the three DOC zones of the Prenestina and Ciociaria hills southeast of Rome. Aleatico makes a Port-like dessert wine on the northern shores of Lake Bolsena at Gradoli.

Cabernet and Merlot are the stars of a number of highly praised modern reds of Latium which prove that the fortunes of premium wine production are not confined to whites.

Rome (Roma), Italy's capital, is also the administrative center of Latium, whose other provinces are Frosinone, Latina, Rieti and Viterbo. The region ranks 9th in size (17,207 square kilometers) and 3rd in population (5,255,000).

Vineyards cover 38,730 hectares, of which registered DOC plots total 16,700 hectares.

Average annual wine production of 3,500,000 hectoliters (6th) includes about 15% DOC, of which 95% is white.

Latium (Lazio)

DOC

1 Aleatico di Gradoli
2 Aprilia
3 Atina
4 Bianco Capena
5 Castelli Romani
6 Cerveteri
7 Cesanese del Piglio or Piglio
8 Cesanese di Affile or Affile
9 Cesanese di Olevano Romano or
   Olevano Romano
10 Circeo
11 Colli Albani
12 Colli della Sabina

13 Colli Etruschi Viterbesi
14 Colli Lanuvini
15 Cori
16 Est! Est!! Est!!! di Montefiascone
17 Frascati
18 Genazzano
19 Marino
20 Montecompatri Colonna
21 Orvieto
22 Tarquinia
23 Velletri
24 Vignanello
25 Zagarolo

DOC (25)

Aleatico di Gradoli : R-Sw; Liquoroso R-Sw-Ft, Rs Ag-2

Aprilia : Merlot R-Dr; Sangiovese R-Dr; Trebbiano W-Dr

Atina : Rosso R-Dr, Rs Ag-2; Cabernet R-Dr, Rs Ag-2

Bianco Capena : W-Dr, also Superiore

Castelli Romani : Bianco W-Dr/Fz, Rosato P-Dr/Fz; Rosso R-Dr/Fz, also Novello

Cerveteri : Bianco W-Dr/Fz/Sw; Rosato P-Dr; Rosso R-Dr/Sw, also Novello

Cesanese del Pigio or Piglio : Secco R-Dr/Fz/Sp or Amabile R-Sw/Fz/Sp or Dolce R-Sw/Fz/Sp

Cesanese di Affile or Affile : Secco R-Dr/Fz/Sp or Amabile R-Sw/Fz/Sp or Dolce R-Sw/Fz/Sp

Cesanese di Olevano Romano or Olevano Romano : Secco R-Dr/Fz/Sp or Amabile R-Sw/Fz/Sp or Dolce R-Sw/Fz/Sp

Circeo : Bianco W-Dr; Rosato P-Dr; Rosso R-Dr, also Novello; Sangiovese R-Dr; Sangiovese Rosato P-Dr; Trebbiano W-Dr

Colli Albani : W-Dr/Sp, also Novello and Superiore

Colli della Sabina : Bianco W-Dr/Fz/Sp; Rosato P-Dr/Fz; Rosso R-Dr/Fz/Sp, also Novello

Colli Etruschi Viterbesi : Bianco W-Dr/Fz; Rosato P-Dr/Fz; Rosso R-Dr/Fz, also Novello; Canaiolo R-Dr; Grechetto W-Dr/Fz, also Novello; Greghetto R-Dr; Merlot R-Dr; Moscatello W-Sw/Fz, also Novello; Moscatello Passito W-Sw; Procanico W-Dr/Fz; Rossetto W-Dr; Sangiovese Rosato P-Dr/Fz; Violone R-Dr

Colli Lanuvini : W-Dr, also Superiore

Cori : Bianco W-Dr; Rosso R-Dr

Est! Est!! Est!!! di Montefiascone : W-Dr/Sp, also Amabile W-Sw/Sp

Frascati : W-Dr, also Novello and Superiore; Amabile and Cannellino W-Sw; Spumante W-Dr-Sp

Genazzano : Bianco W-Dr, also Novello; Rosso R-Dr, also Novello

Marino : W-Dr, also Superiore; Spumante W-Dr-Sp

Montecompatri Colonna : W-Dr/Fz, also Superiore

Orvieto (shared with Umbria) : W-Dr, also Superiore

Tarquinia : Bianco W-Dr/Fz, also Amabile W-Sw; Rosato P-Dr; Rosso R-Dr, also Novello and Amabile R-Sw

Velletri : Bianco W-Dr, also Superiore; Rosso R-Dr, Rs Ag-2; Spumante W-Dr-Sp

Vignanello : Bianco W-Dr, also Superiore; Rosato P-Dr; Rosso R-Dr, Rs Ag-2, also Novello; Greco W-Dr/Sp

Zagarolo : W-Dr, also Superiore

IGT (5)

Civitella d'Agliano
Colli Cimini
Frusinante
Lazio
Nettuno

Molise

The often overlooked region of Molise, which was once an appendix of Abruzzi, gained official status in wine in the 1980s with the DOCs of Biferno and Pentro di Isernia. The undeniable aptitude for vines on the sunny hillsides between the Apennines and the Adriatic indicates that with a little more effort Molise's wine producers could match on a small scale the quality of their neighbors in Abruzzi, Apulia or Campania.

The recent DOC of Molise takes in a number of Italian and native varieties, creating new possibilities for producers who are striving to establish an identity with wine beyond the region. The rolling hills and the mild Adriatic climate of Molise favor wines of class, though the evidence in bottle has been scarce so far.

The IGT category of Osco or Terre degli Osci refers to the Oscan people who inhabited Molise in prehistoric times. The other IGT category is Rotae.

Campobasso is the administrative center of Molise, whose other province is Isernia. The region ranks 19th in both size (4,438 square kilometers) and population (329,000).

Vineyards cover 9,000 hectares, of which registered DOC plots total 350 hectares.

Average annual wine production of 330,000 hectoliters (18th) includes 4.5% DOC, some 75% of which is red.

DOC (3)

Biferno : Bianco W-Dr; Rosato P-Dr; Rosso R-Dr, Rs Ag-3

Molise : Novello R-Dr; Aglianico R-Dr/Fz, Rs Ag-2; Cabernet Sauvignon R-Dr/Fz; Chardonnay WDr/Fz/Sp; Falanghina W-Dr/Fz; Greco Bianco W-Dr/Fz; Montepulciano R-Dr/Fz, Rs Ag-2; Moscato W-Sw/Fz/Sp; Pinot Bianco W-Dr/Fz/Sp; Sangiovese R-Dr/Fz; Sauvignon W-Dr/Fz; Tintilia R-Dr/Fz, Rs Ag-2; Trebbiano W-Dr/Fz

Pentro di Isernia : Bianco W-Dr; Rosato P-Dr; Rosso R-Dr

IGT (2)

Osco or Terre degli Osci
Rotae

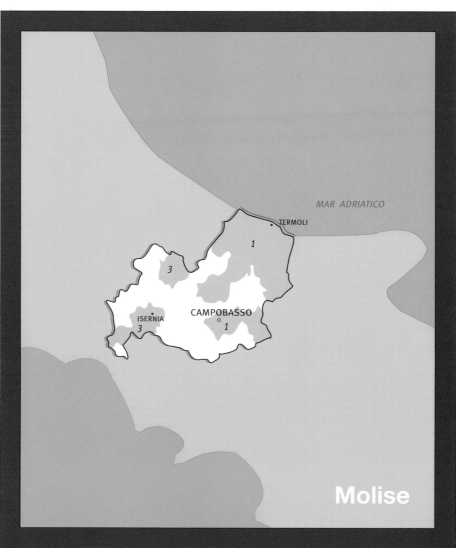

MAR ADRIATICO

TERMOLI

1

3

ISERNIA

CAMPOBASSO

1

3

Molise

DOC

1 Biferno
2 Molise*
3 Pentro di Isernia

*Wines may be produced throughout the region

Abruzzi (Abruzzo)

L'Aquila is the administrative center of Abruzzi, whose other provinces include Chieti, Pescara and Teramo. The region ranks 13th in size (10,798 square kilometers) and 14th in population (1,277,000).

Vineyards cover 33,300 hectares, of which registered DOC plots total 11,500 hectares.

Average annual wine production of 4,000,000 hectoliters (5th) includes 19%DOC, of which about two-thirds is red.

In a nation of myriad appellations, Abruzzi offers wine drinkers refreshing simplicity. The long-standing region-wide DOCs for Montepulciano and Trebbiano d'Abruzzo have been complemented by an appellation for Controguerra, which takes in 12 types of wine.

Abruzzi, which is two-thirds mountains and one-third hills, boasts highly favorable natural conditions for grapevines. Growers favor the predominant Montepulciano and Trebbiano, while growing some highly productive vines (the region has Italy's highest average yields) for bulk wines and table grapes, and experimenting in an increasingly convincing way with outside varieties.

Despite the outward simplicity of the region's DOC system, certain details of Abruzzi's production are worth pointing out. The native Montepulciano (not to be confused with the town of that name in Tuscany where Vino Nobile is made) is a vine of convincing character that has been winning admirers abroad.

In parts of the Abruzzi, notably in the low hills of the northern province of Teramo (where it can be referred to as Colline Teramane), Montepulciano becomes a red of irresistible character—full-bodied, even robust, with a capacity to age but with such supple smoothness that it can be eminently drinkable even when young. In higher inland areas, or from vineyards where growers have the habit of high yields, the wines tend to be lighter, often better suited to Cerasuolo, a sturdy cherry-colored rosé.

Most Trebbiano is based on the prolific Tuscan variety, which makes light, rather acidic whites of subtle aroma and flavor. A few growers work with the "true" Trebbiano d'Abruzzo (which may or may not be related to the Bombino Bianco of Apulia). A choice few have managed to make Trebbiano of remarkable depth and texture, with a propensity to develop complexity with four or five years, sometimes even more, of aging. But those fine wines are not easy to find.

DOC (3)

IGT (9)

Controguerra : Bianco W-Dr/Fz; Rosso R-Dr, Rs Ag-2, also Novello; Passito W/R-Sw Ag-1; Passito Annoso W/R-Sw Ag-3; Spumante W-Dr-Sp; Cabernet R-Dr; Chardonnay W-Dr; Ciliegiolo R-Dr; Malvasia W-Dr; Merlot R-Dr; Moscato Amabile W-Sw; Passerina W-Dr; Pinot Nero R-Dr; Riesling W-Dr

Montepulciano d'Abruzzo (Colline Teramane) : Cerasuolo P-Dr; Rosso R-Dr, Rs Ag-2, Montepulciano d'Abruzzo Colline Teramane Ag-2, Rs Ag-3

Trebbiano d'Abruzzo : W-Dr

Alto Tirino

Colli Aprutini

Colli del Sangro

Colline Frentane

Colline Pescaresi

Colline Teatine

Del Vastese or Historium

Terre di Chieti

Valle Peligna

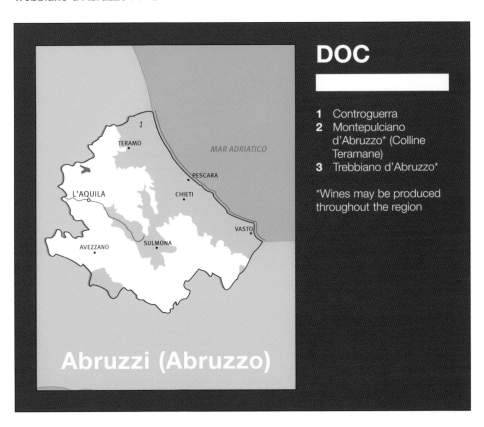

DOC

1 Controguerra
2 Montepulciano d'Abruzzo* (Colline Teramane)
3 Trebbiano d'Abruzzo*

*Wines may be produced throughout the region

Abruzzi (Abruzzo)

Marches (Marche)

Ancona is the administrative center of the Marches, whose other provinces are Ascoli Piceno, Macerata and Pesaro-Urbino. The region ranks 15th in size (9,694 square kilometers) and 13th in population (1,455,000).

Vineyards cover 24,900 hectares, of which registered DOC plots total 10,400 hectares.

Average annual wine production of 1,670,000 hectoliters (10th) includes 25% DOC, of which more than 70% is white.

Verdicchio is the plenipotentiary of the wines of this pleasant Adriatic region, whose long-time devotion to whites no longer obscures the increasing merits of its reds.

The Castelli di Jesi DOC zone, covering a vast tract of hills west of the port of Ancona, is the home of the Verdicchio that made an early impression abroad in its green amphora bottles. But recently producers have created a new image of Verdicchio as a white wine of special character that comes across even more convincingly in standard bottles.

Class has risen so steadily that even wine still sold in the hourglass-shaped amphora seems a cut above the general level of popular whites. Verdicchio dei Castelli di Jesi Classico, has been described as Italy's premier wine to serve with fish. Some producers make wines that develop such impressive depth and complexity with age that Verdicchio is increasingly ranked among the noblest native white varieties of Italy.

Verdicchio di Matelica, grown in limited quantities in a mountainous zone, can have more body and strength than wines from Jesi. Verdicchio from both DOC zones makes convincing sparkling wine as well, usually by the sealed tank method of fermentation, but also occasionally by the classical method in bottle.

The recent Esino DOC, which coincides with parts of the two Verdicchio zones, provides for red and white wines, usually fresh and fruity. The region's other white wines, notably Bianchello del Metauro and Falerio dei Colli Ascolani, are usually light and zesty and also go nicely with seafood.

The red wines of the Marches are based chiefly on Sangiovese and Montepulciano—sometimes blended, sometimes not. The most important in terms of volume is Rosso Piceno, dominated by Sangiovese. It comes from a DOC zone covering much of the eastern flank of the region, stretching from the superiore area between Ascoli Piceno and the sea north through the coastal hills to Senigallia.

Rosso Conero, dominated by Montepulciano, has gained even more praise, thanks to the devotion to quality shown by its leading producers. It originates in a zone on the slopes of the Conero massif south of Ancona. Both Rosso Conero and Rosso Piceno were habitually made to drink within two to four years, when they are persuasively round and fresh in flavor, though certain producers have made wines that age remarkably well from good vintages—sometimes for a decade or more.

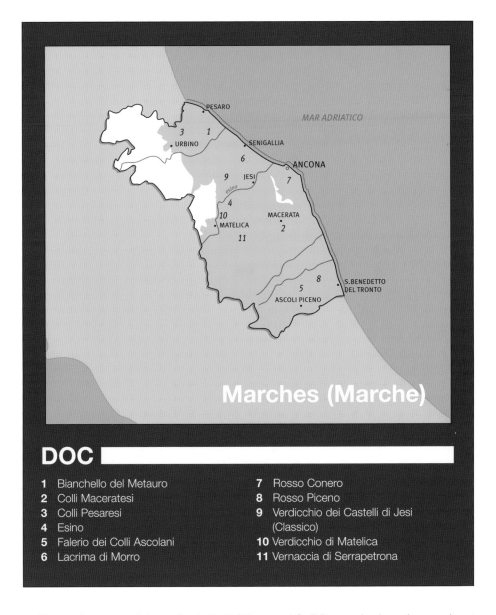

Marches (Marche)

DOC

1. Bianchello del Metauro
2. Colli Maceratesi
3. Colli Pesaresi
4. Esino
5. Falerio dei Colli Ascolani
6. Lacrima di Morro
7. Rosso Conero
8. Rosso Piceno
9. Verdicchio dei Castelli di Jesi (Classico)
10. Verdicchio di Matelica
11. Vernaccia di Serrapetrona

The northern part of the region is the DOC zone of Colli Pesaresi, where the prominent wine is a Sangiovese, which bears a strong family resemblance to the wines of that variety of neighboring Romagna.

Although the emphasis remains strongly on native vines, recent results with such outside varieties as Cabernet Sauvignon, Merlot, Chardonnay and Sauvignon have shown eminent promise in the temperate hills of the Marches.

DOC (11)

Bianchello del Metauro : W-Dr

Colli Maceratesi : W-Dr

Colli Pesaresi : Bianco W-Dr; Rosso R-Dr, also Novello; Focara Rosso R-Dr; Roncaglia Bianco W-Dr; Sangiovese R-Dr, also Novello

Esino : Bianco W-Dr/Fz; Rosso R-Dr, also Novello

Falerio dei Colli Ascolani : W-Dr

Lacrima di Morro : R-Dr/Sw

Rosso Conero : R-Dr, Rs Ag-2.5

Rosso Piceno : R-Dr, Sup Ag-1, also Novello

Verdicchio dei Castelli di Jesi (Classico) : W-Dr, Rs Ag-2; Classico, also Sup, Rs Ag-2; Passito W-Sw Ag-1; Spumante W-Dr-Sp, Rs Ag-1

Verdicchio di Matelica : W-Dr, Rs Ag-2; Passito W-Sw Ag-1; Spumante W-Dr-Sp

Vernaccia di Serrapetrona : R-Dr/Sw-Sp

IGT (1)

Marche

Umbria

Umbria has long been renowned for white wine, thanks mainly to the historical prominence of Orvieto. But evidence is now irrefutable that the scenic hills of the "green heart of Italy" have an aptitude for a multitude of varieties, white and red, native and foreign. The region's two DOCG wines—Montefalco Sagrantino and Torgiano Rosso Riserva—are red.

Orvieto was once the most celebrated of Italian whites as a semisweet or abboccato wine, praised by the popes, princes and painters who sojourned in the hill town north of Rome with its splendid cathedral and sweeping views over the Umbrian landscape. But as tastes changed Orvieto was modified from a soft, golden wine into a pale, pure, crisp creature of modern enology.

Modern Orvieto is a commercial success as one of Italy's best-selling DOC whites with a solid following abroad. Recently, some producers have achieved more character in the wine through lower grape yields and more meticulous selection and by letting the grape skins remain in contact with the juice for a while before fermentation. Just lately Orvieto's abboccato and amabile versions have made a comeback as dessert wines.

Although Procanico (a local species of Trebbiano) and Malvasia prevail in Orvieto, growers in the zone have been working successfully with such outside varieties as Chardonnay, Sauvignon and the Pinots, as well as the admirable local Grechetto. Red wine from the area is now covered by the DOCs of Rosso Orvietano and Lago di Corbara.

The most prestigious Umbrian wine is the red Torgiano Rosso riserva, which has special status as DOCG (though Torgiano DOC appellation covers a range of other wines). A modern classic based on Sangiovese, Torgiano Rosso riserva, under the name Rubesco, has been known to age to unique splendor for two decades or more.

Sagrantino, an ancient variety grown only around the hill town of Montefalco, is an intriguing native that makes both dry and sweet wines of unmistakable grandeur. It, too, has been granted a special DOCG, separate from the DOC Montefalco for lighter red and white wines.

Among the many outside varieties planted in Umbria, Merlot and Barbera have been prominent for more than a century. More recently, Cabernet Sauvignon and Chardonnay have shown promise in varietal wines and in blends. Even Pinot Nero has given indications of more than the usual class here.

Perugia is the administrative center of Umbria, whose other province is Terni. The region ranks 16th in size (8,456 square kilometers) and 17th in population (833,000).

Vineyards cover 16,500 hectares, of which registered DOC or DOCG plots total 6,400 hectares.

Average annual wine production of 960,000 hectoliters (15th) includes 23% DOC or DOCG, of which about 60% is white.

Umbria

DOCG

1 Montefalco Sagrantino or Sagrantino di Montefalco
2 Torgiano Rosso Riserva

DOC

3 Assisi
4 Colli Altotiberini
5 Colli Amerini
6 Colli del Trasimeno or Trasimeno
7 Colli Martani
8 Colli Perugini
9 Lago di Corbara
10 Montefalco
11 Orvieto and Orvieto Classico
12 Rosso Orvietano or Orvietano Rosso
13 Torgiano

Umbria has numerous curiosities among its vines and wines, though few of the local rarities ever leave the region. Vin Santo, pressed from semidried Grechetto or Malvasia grapes, is usually sweet and most prized by Umbrians as a wine for any occasion.

DOCG (2)

Montefalco Sagrantino or Sagrantino di Montefalco : Secco R-Dr Ag-3; Passito R-Sw Ag-3

Torgiano Rosso Riserva : R-Dr Ag-3

DOC (11)

Assisi : Bianco W-Dr; Rosato P-Dr; Rosso R-Dr, also Novello

Colli Altotiberini : Bianco W-Dr; Rosato P-Dr; Rosso R-Dr

Colli Amerini : Bianco W-Dr; Rosato P-Dr; Rosso R-Dr, also Novello and Sup; Malvasia W-Dr

Colli del Trasimeno or Trasimeno : Bianco W-Dr/Fz, also Bianco Scelto; Rosato P-Dr; Rosso R-Dr, also Novello and Rosso Scelto Ag-1, Rs Ag-2; Spumante Classico W-Sp; Vin Santo W-Sw Ag-1.5; Cabernet Sauvignon R-Dr, Rs Ag-2; Gamay R-Dr, Rs Ag-2; Grechetto W-Dr; Merlot R-Dr, Rs Ag-2

Colli Martani : Grechetto W-Dr; Grechetto di Todi W-Dr; Sangiovese R-Dr Ag-1, Rs Ag-2; Trebbiano W-Dr

Colli Perugini : Bianco W-Dr; Rosato P-Dr; Rosso R-Dr, also Novello; Spumante W-Sp; Vin Santo W-Sw; Chardonnay W-Dr; Cabernet Sauvignon R-Dr; Grechetto W-Dr; Merlot R-Dr; Pinot Grigio W-Dr; Sangiovese R-Dr; Trebbiano W-Dr

Lago di Corbara : Rosso R-Dr Ag-1; Cabernet Sauvignon R-Dr Ag-1; Merlot R-Dr Ag-1; Pinot Nero R-Dr Ag-1

Montefalco : Bianco W-Dr; Rosso R-Dr Ag-1.5, Rs Ag-2.5

Orvieto (shared with Latium) and Orvieto Classico : W-Dr, also Sup W-Dr/Sw; Orvieto Classico W-Dr, also Sup W-Dr/Sw (Classico applies to wines from the original zone in Umbria)

Rosso Orvietano or Orvietano Rosso : R-Dr; Aleatico R-Sw; Cabernet R-Dr; Cabernet Franc R-Dr; Cabernet Sauvignon R-Dr; Canaiolo R-Dr; Ciliegiolo R-Dr; Merlot R-Dr; Pinot Nero R-Dr; Sangiovese R-Dr

Torgiano : Bianco W-Dr; Rosato P-Dr; Rosso R-Dr Ag-1; Spumante W-Sp Ag-2; Chardonnay W-Dr; Cabernet Sauvignon R-Dr Ag-1; Pinot Grigio W-Dr; Pinot Nero R-Dr Ag-1; Riesling Italico W-Dr

IGT (6)

Allerona

Bettona

Cannara

Narni

Spello

Umbria

Tuscany (Toscana)

Florence (Firenze) is the administrative center of Tuscany, whose provinces include Arezzo, Grosseto, Livorno, Lucca, Massa-Carrara, Pisa, Pistoia, Prato and Siena. The region ranks 5th in size (22,997 square kilometers) and 9th in population (3,529,000).

Vineyards cover 85,000 hectares, of which registered DOC or DOCG plots total 35,000 hectares.

Average annual wine production of 2,550,000 hectoliters (8th) includes about 55% DOC or DOCG, of which more than 80% is red.

Florence's region continues to advance its position as the nation's most dynamic producer of premium wines, following decades of turning out popular Chianti in straw-covered flasks. Tuscany's modern renaissance in wine began in Chianti, in the central hills around Siena and Florence, but it rapidly spread to take in the strip along the Mediterranean coast that was not previously noted for vineyards.

Much of the progress has come with classical reds based on the native Sangiovese vine—Chianti, Brunello di Montalcino, Vino Nobile di Montepulciano and Carmignano—all DOCG. But growing success with other reds (especially the stylish non-DOC wines known as "Super Tuscans") has been augmented by new styles of whites to enhance the region's reputation.

Chianti, still the dominant force in Tuscan viniculture, has long rated as the most Italian of wines. This is partly because it is the most voluminous and widely sold classified wine, but also because it has a personality that cannot be pinned down. Its multifarious nature is quintessentially Italian.

Chianti is produced in eight distinct zones and adjacent areas that cover a vast territory of central Tuscany around the original core of Chianti Classico. In those gorgeously rugged hills variations in soil and climate contribute as much to the individuality of each authentic estate wine as do winemakers' quests for creative styles. Some Chianti is still fairly fresh, easy and quaffable, though a growing portion is rich and elaborate and capable of becoming aristocratic with age. Those variables can be confusing, but for consumers who persist, Chianti offers some of the best value in wine today.

Much Chianti is identified by its subdistricts, most prominently Classico, whose producers' consortium is symbolized by a black rooster. Many estates also emphasize the name of a special vineyard as a mark of distinction. What Chianti has in common with all of the traditional red wines of Tuscany is its major grape variety Sangiovese.

In the past varieties were often blended, but today the emphasis is strongly on Sangiovese or Sangioveto, which deserves to be ranked with Italy's and the world's noblest vines. From good vintages, pure Sangiovese wines are rich in body and intricate in flavor with deep ruby-garnet colors. Some are smooth and round almost from the start, but others need years to develop the nuances of bouquet and flavor unique to well-aged Tuscan reds.

Tuscany (Toscana)

DOCG

1. Brunello di Montalcino
2. Carmignano Rosso Riserva
3. Chianti (A Colli Aretini, B Colli Fiorentini, C Colli Senesi, D Colline Pisane, E Montalbano, F Montespertoli, G Rufina)
4. Chianti Classico
5. Vernaccia di San Gimignano
6. Vino Nobile di Montepulciano

DOC

7. Ansonica Costa dell'Argentario
8. Barco Reale di Carmignano
9. Bianco della Valdinievole
10. Bianco dell'Empolese
11. Bianco di Pitigliano
12. Bianco Pisano di San Torpè
13. Bolgheri (Sassicaia)
14. Candia dei Colli Apuani
15. Capalbio
16. Carmignano
17. Colli dell'Etruria Centrale
18. Colli di Luni
19. Colline Lucchesi
20. Cortona
21. Elba
22. Montecarlo
23. Montecucco
24. Monteregio di Massa Marittima
25. Montescudaio
26. Morellino di Scansano
27. Moscadello di Montalcino
28. Orcia
29. Parrina
30. Pomino
31. Rosso di Montalcino
32. Rosso di Montepulciano
33. San Gimignano
34. Sant'Antimo
35. Sovana
36. Val d'Arbia
37. Valdichiana
38. Val di Cornia (Campiglia Marittima, Piombino, San Vincenzo, Suvereto)
39. Vin Santo del Chianti (A Colli Aretini, B Colli Fiorentini, C Colli Senesi, D Colline Pisane, E Montalbano, F Montespertoli, G Rufina)
40. Vin Santo del Chianti Classico
41. Vin Santo di Montepulciano

Tuscany's appellation of greatest stature is Brunello di Montalcino, a DOCG from a fortress town south of Siena where reds of legendary power and longevity have commanded lofty prices. Conceived by the Biondi Santi family a century ago, Brunello is now issued under more than a hundred labels, representing small farms, established estates and even international corporations. Brunello producers also make the DOCs of Rosso di Montalcino (a younger wine from Sangiovese), the sweet white Moscadello di Montalcino (from Moscato) and a range of wines that carry the appellation Sant'Antimo.

Not far from Montalcino is Montepulciano with its Vino Nobile, made from a type of Sangiovese known as Prugnolo Gentile. The nobile entered the name centuries ago, apparently in homage to its status among the nobility. The poet Francesco Redi described Montepulciano's red as "king of all wines." After a lapse of decades, Vino Nobile has made an impressive comeback under DOCG and is once again living up to its name. Producers may also produce the DOC Rosso di Montepulciano as a younger alternative to Vino Nobile.

Carmignano rates special mention as a wine singled out for protection by the Grand Duke of Tuscany in 1716. Today this rare red from Sangiovese and Cabernet ranks as DOCG, though the red Barco Reale and other wines of Carmignano remain as DOC.

Pomino, which was also cited in the decree of 1716, is a high altitude DOC zone with a red that blends Sangiovese with Cabernet and Merlot and a special white which includes Chardonnay and Pinot. Among numerous other DOC reds, Morellino di Scansano, grown in the coastal hills of the Maremma, is strongly on the rise.

The production of upscale alternative wines, which began as a trend in the 1970s, became an essential factor in the general improvement of Tuscan reds. Cult wines which have become known as "Super Tuscans" continue to prosper.

Yet Sassicaia, the pure Cabernet that in the 1970s convinced the world that Italy could make modern reds of international appeal, now has a DOC of its own under the Bolgheri appellation. The Sangiovese-Cabernet blend of Tignanello served as the model for Tuscany's new style of red wine aged in small oak barrels or barriques instead of ancient casks. Then came Cabernet-Sangiovese blends and, later, reds from Merlot, Syrah and Pinot Nero.

The "Super Tuscans" rank among the most esteemed and expensive red wines of Italy. Today those that remain outside of DOC/DOCG are generally entitled to the regionwide Toscana IGT.

Inspired by the success of Cabernet and Merlot in Bolgheri, wines from the coastal sector of Tuscany have risen rapidly in prestige to challenge the central hills for supremacy. In the heart of the Maremma, as the coastal hills of southwestern Tuscany are known, lies the Morellino di Scansano zone, source of a red based on Sangiovese. Other DOC zones of promise include Val di Cornia, Montecucco, Monteregio di Massa Marittima, Montescudaio, Capalbio and Sovana.

The pride of many a Tuscan winemaker is the rich Vin Santo, which has become DOC in many zones around the region. Pressed from partly dried grapes and aged in small wooden barrels, Vin Santo can be an exquisite dessert or aperitif wine. Most Vin Santo is made from white varieties, mainly Malvasia and Trebbiano, though the type called Occhio di Pernice comes from red wine grapes.

Until recently, Tuscan whites rarely enjoyed much prestige, probably because most of them consisted of the pedestrian varieties of Trebbiano and Malvasia. Exceptions to the rule stand out from the crowd. Vernaccia di San Gimignano, from the ancient Vernaccia vine, has enjoyed a revival that led to its promotion as the region's first white DOCG. Vermentino has spread through the coastal hills as a white variety of outstanding promise.

Recently, whites of depth and complexity have been produced in Tuscany, made from such international varieties as Chardonnay, Sauvignon and Pinot Bianco and Grigio, all of which are finding comfortable environments in cooler parts of the region's hills.

DOCG (6)

Brunello di Montalcino : R-Dr Ag-5, also Vigna, Rs Ag-6

Carmignano Rosso Riserva : R-Dr Ag-3

Chianti (Colli Aretini, Colli Fiorentini, Colli Senesi, Colline Pisane, Montalbano, Montespertoli, Rufina) : R-Dr, also Sup, Rs Ag-2

Chianti Classico : R-Dr Ag-1, Rs Ag-2

Vernaccia di San Gimignano : W-Dr, Rs Ag-1

Vino Nobile di Montepulciano : R-Dr Ag-2, Rs Ag-3

DOC (35)

Ansonica Costa dell'Argentario : W-Dr

Barco Reale di Carmignano : R-Dr

Bianco della Valdinievole : W-Dr; Vin Santo W-Dr/Sw Ag-3

Bianco dell'Empolese : W-Dr; Vin Santo W-Dr/Sw Ag-3

Bianco di Pitigliano : W-Dr, also Sup; Spumante W-Dr-Sp

Bianco Pisano di San Torpè : W-Dr; Vin Santo W-Dr/Sw Ag-3, Rs Ag-4

Bolgheri (Sassicaia) : Bianco W-Dr; Rosato P-Dr; Rosso R-Dr; Rosso Sup Ag-2; Sassicaia R-Dr Ag-2; Vin Santo Occhio di Pernice R-Sw Ag-3, Rs Ag-4; Sauvignon W-Dr; Vermentino W-Dr

Candia dei Colli Apuani : W-Dr/Sw/Fz; Vin Santo W-Sw Ag-3

Capalbio : Bianco W-Dr; Rosato P-Dr; Rosso R-Dr, Rs Ag-3; Vin Santo R-Dr/Sw Ag-3; Sauvignon W-Dr; Cabernet Sauvignon R-Dr; Sangiovese R-Dr; Vermentino W-Dr

Carmignano : Rosato P-Dr; Vin Santo W-Sw Ag-3, Rs Ag-4; Vin Santo Occhio di Pernice R-Sw Ag-3, Rs Ag-4

Colli dell'Etruria Centrale : Bianco W-Dr; Rosato P-Dr; Rosso or Vermiglio R-Dr, also Novello; Vin Santo W-Dr/Sw Ag-3, Rs Ag-4; Vin Santo Occhio di Pernice R-Sw Ag-3, Rs Ag-4

Colli di Luni (shared with Liguria) : Bianco W-Dr; Rosso R-Dr, Rs Ag-2; Vermentino W-Dr

Colline Lucchesi : Bianco W-Dr; Rosso R-Dr, Rs Ag-2; Vin Santo W-Dr/Sw Ag-3; Vin Santo Occhio di Pernice R-Sw Ag-3; Merlot R-Dr, Rs Ag-2; Sangiovese R-Dr, Rs Ag-2; Sauvignon W-Dr; Vermentino W-Dr

Cortona : Rosato P-Dr; Vin Santo W-Dr/Sw Ag-3, Rs Ag-5; Vin Santo Occhio di Pernice R-Sw Ag-8; Cabernet Sauvignon R-Dr; Chardonnay W-Dr; Grechetto W-Dr; Gamay R-Dr; Merlot R-Dr; Pinot Bianco W-Dr; Pinot Nero R-Dr; Riesling Italico W-Dr; Sangiovese R-Dr; Sauvignon W-Dr; Syrah R-Dr. (All types may refer to a vineyard or Vigna)

Elba : Bianco W-Dr; Bianco Spumante W-Dr-Sp; Rosato P-Dr; Rosso R-Dr, Rs Ag-2; Vin Santo W-Dr/Sw Ag-3, Rs Ag-4; Vin Santo Occhio di Pernice R-Sw Ag-3; Aleatico R-Sw; Ansonica W-Dr; Ansonica Passito W-Sw; Moscato W-Sw

Montecarlo : Bianco W-Dr; Rosso R-Dr, Rs Ag-2; Vin Santo W-Dr/Sw Ag-3; Vin Santo Occhio di Pernice R-Sw Ag-3, Rs Ag-4

Montecucco : Bianco W-Dr; Rosso R-Dr, Rs Ag-2; Sangiovese R-Dr, Rs Ag-2; Vermentino W-Dr

Monteregio di Massa Marittima : Bianco W-Dr; Rosato P-Dr; Rosso R-Dr, Rs Ag-2, also Novello; Vermentino W-Dr; Vin Santo W-Dr/Sw Ag-3; Vin Santo Occhio di Pernice R-Sw Ag-3, Rs Ag-4

Montescudaio : Bianco W-Dr; Rosso R-Dr, Rs Ag-2; Vin Santo W-Sw Ag-4; Cabernet R-Dr, Rs Ag-2; Chardonnay W-Dr; Merlot R-Dr, Rs Ag-2; Sangiovese R-Dr, Rs Ag-2; Sauvignon W-Dr; Vermentino W-Dr

Morellino di Scansano : R-Dr, Rs Ag-2

Moscadello di Montalcino : W-Sw/Fz; Vendemmia Tardiva W-Sw

Orcia : Bianco W-Dr, also Vigna; Novello R-Dr; Rosso R-Dr, also Vigna; Vin Santo W-Sw Ag-3

Parrina : Bianco W-Dr; Rosato P-Dr; Rosso R-Dr, Rs Ag-2

Pomino : Bianco W-Dr; Rosso R-Dr, Rs Ag-3; Vin Santo W/R-Sw Ag-3

Rosso di Montalcino : R-Dr, also Vigna

Rosso di Montepulciano : R-Dr

San Gimignano : Rosato P-Dr; Rosso R-Dr, Rs Ag-2, also Novello; Cabernet Sauvignon R-Dr; Chardonnay W-Dr; Sangiovese Rosato P-Dr; Vin Santo W-Sw Ag-3; Vin Santo Occhio di Pernice R-Sw Ag-3

Sant'Antimo : Bianco W-Dr; Rosso R-Dr, also Novello; Vin Santo W-Dr/Sw Ag-3, Rs Ag-4; Vin Santo Occhio di Pernice R-Sw Ag-3, Rs Ag-4; Cabernet Sauvignon; Chardonnay W-Dr; Merlot R-Dr; Pinot Grigio W-Dr; Pinot Nero R-Dr; Sauvignon W-Dr

Sovana : Rosato P-Dr; Rosso, also Sup, Rs Ag-2.5; Aleatico Sup R-Sw, Rs Ag-2.4; Cabernet Sauvignon Sup R-Dr, Rs Ag-2.5; Merlot Sup R-Dr, Rs Ag-2.5; Sangiovese Sup R-Dr, Rs Ag-2.5

Val d'Arbia : W-Dr; Vin Santo W-Dr/Sw Ag-3

Valdichiana : Bianco or Bianco Vergine W-Dr; Rosato P-Dr; Rosso R-Dr; Vin Santo W-Dr/Sw Ag-3, Rs Ag-4; Chardonnay W-Dr; Grechetto W-Dr; Sangiovese R-Dr

Val di Cornia (Campiglia Marittima, Piombino, San Vincenzo, Suvereto) : Bianco W-Dr; Rosato P-Dr; Rosso R-Dr, Rs Ag-3

Vin Santo del Chianti (Colli Aretini, Colli Fiorentini, Colli Senesi, Colline Pisane, Montalbano, Montespertoli, Rufina) : W-Dr/Sw Ag-3, Rs Ag-4; Occhio di Pernice R-Sw Ag-3, Rs Ag-4

Vin Santo del Chianti Classico : W-Dr/Sw Ag-3, Rs Ag-4; Occhio di Pernice R-Sw Ag-3

Vin Santo di Montepulciano : W-Sw Ag-3, Rs Ag-5; Occhio di Pernice R-Sw Ag-8

IGT (5)

Alta Valle della Greve

Colli della Toscana Centrale

Maremma Toscana

Toscana or Toscano

Val di Magra

North by Northwest: From the Adriatic to Mont Blanc

Emilia-Romagna, Liguria, Lombardy, Piedmont, Valle d'Aosta

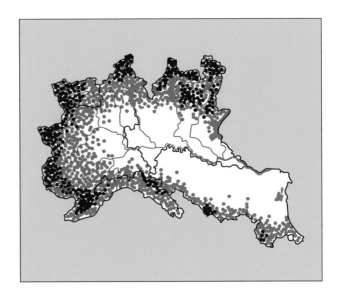

The five regions of north-central and northwestern Italy cover much of the great arc of the Alps and Apennines that walls in the Po as it flows east through its broad valley to the Adriatic. The types of wine—like the topography, soil and climate—vary to extremes in these regions, which are grouped rather loosely as neighbors but, in true Italian style, maintain their own proud identities.

This most affluent part of Italy comprises the "industrial triangle" between Milan, Turin and the Mediterranean port of Genoa and the agriculturally fluent flatlands of the Po and its tributaries. Since property is valuable and mountains take up a major share of space, vineyards are confined and wine is a commodity that must be either financially or spiritually rewarding. Yet between the cool terraces of the Alps and the often torrid fields of the Po basin, contrasts abound. Along with some of Italy's most revered bottles can be found some of its most frivolous. But whether the label says Barolo or Lambrusco, the winemaker no doubt takes his work seriously.

Between them, the five regions produce about 20 percent of Italy's total wine but account for more than a quarter of the DOC.

Emilia-Romagna contributes heavily with the fourth largest output among regions after Veneto, Sicily and Apulia. Piedmont stands tall in the quality field with the most DOC and DOCG zones of any region, even though it ranks only seventh in over all production.

Still, Piedmont dwarfs its neighbors of Valle d'Aosta and Liguria, which, by Italian standards at least, are mere dabblers in wine. Valle d'Aosta, the smallest region, produces by far the least volume of wine from its rocky slopes. Its DOC output is surpassed by some single wineries in other regions. Liguria, with little space for vines between the mountains and the Mediterranean, is second from the last in production, offering wines that are rarely more than esoteric.

Despite the proximity of France, whose vines have been warmly welcomed elsewhere in Italy, growers in Piedmont, Valle d'Aosta and Liguria prefer their own vines and tend to make wine in their own style. Piedmont's host of worthy natives includes Barbera, Dolcetto, Grignolino, Freisa, Cortese, Arneis, Brachetto, the Canelli clone of Moscato (for Asti Spumante) and the noblest of them all in Nebbiolo (source of Barolo, Barbaresco and Gattinara).

The vines of Valle d'Aosta often have French names—Petit Rouge, Gros Vien, Blanc de Valdigne, for instance—due to the Savoyard history of the region. Liguria favors the local Rossese, Pigato and Vermentino, while working with its own version of Dolcetto, known as Ormeasco.

Lombardy, the most populous region, ranks only twelfth in wine production, but it does boast a major concentration of Nebbiolo vines for the DOC reds of the mountainous Valtellina and spreads of Chardonnay and Pinot vines for sparkling wines of Franciacorta and Oltrepò Pavese.

Emilia-Romagna had been a leading exporter of wines with shipments to America of sweet and bubbly Lambrusco, whose vines spill over the fertile plains of Emilia. But lately growers have been concentrating on distinctive wines from the hills. Best known are the Albana and Sangiovese of Romagna, but gaining notice are Barbera, Cabernet, Chardonnay and Sauvignon from the Apennine foothills of Emilia.

Emilia-Romagna

Bologna is the administrative center of Emilia-Romagna, whose provinces include Ferrara, Forlì, Modena, Parma, Piacenza, Ravenna, Rimini and Reggio nell'Emilia. The region ranks 6th in size (22,124 square kilometers) and 8th in population (3,960,000).

Vineyards cover 62,290 hectares, of which registered DOC or DOCG plots total 29,925 hectares.

Average annual wine production of 6,830,000 hectoliters (4th) includes about 14% DOC or DOCG, of which about 75% is red.

Emilia-Romagna, as the hyphenated name reveals, consists of two distinct sectors which coincide more or less at the capital of Bologna. To the west lies Emilia, with its prosperous towns strung like jewels along the ancient Emilian Way: Modena, Reggio, Parma, Fidenza, Fiorenzuola, as far as Piacenza on the Po. East of Bologna lies Romagna with the towns of Faenza, Forlì, Cesena, Ferrara, Ravenna and the Adriatic resort of Rimini.

Emilia-Romagna's wines might be considered northern Italy's most eccentric, different on the whole from their neighbors', often facile in style but always refreshingly individualistic.

In Emilia the premier wine is Lambrusco, in frothy shades of purple to pink, made from grapes grown on high trellised vines, mainly in the flatlands south of the Po. Romagna's wines come primarily from the native Sangiovese, Trebbiano and Albana, the variety that accounted for Italy's first white DOCG.

Lambrusco is produced in volume in the four DOC zones around Modena and Reggio, though few consumers abroad have tasted the wine in its authentic dry style. Most Lambrusco shipped away is amabile or sweet, while most of what is drunk at home is dutifully dry and more often than not DOC. Though there are historical precedents for both types, the dry is considered the unparalleled match for the region's rich cooking.

Even the hill wines of Emilia tend to be frothy. Vineyards in the foothills of the Apennines to the south render fun-loving whites made from Malvasia, Trebbiano and Ortrugo and zesty reds from Barbera and Bonarda. But there is a definite trend in the DOC zones of Colli Piacentini, Colli Bolognesi and Colli di Parma to make still and somewhat serious wines from such varieties as Sauvignon, Chardonnay, the Pinots, Barbera, Cabernet and Merlot. Natural conditions favor wines of depth and finesse, but markets seem to favor the lightweights.

Moving into Romagna, the plains of the Po basin between Ferrara and Ravenna are noted for fruit, vegetables and ultra productive vines, most of which are sources of blending wines. The hills south of Imola, Faenza, Forlì, Cesena and Rimini are known for wines from the native Albana, Sangiovese and Trebbiano all of which carry the name Romagna.

Albana di Romagna, which emerged in 1987 as Italy's first DOCG white wine, is most often dry and still with a distinctive almond undertone and occasionally some complexity. Albana's best expression seems to be as a richly sweet passito from partly dried grapes. The traditional semisweet and bubbly versions are usually consumed at home. Romagna's Trebbiano, distinct from other vines of the name, is almost always light and fresh, whether still or bubbly, with a fragility that makes it best in its youth.

The favorite of Romagnans is Sangiovese, usually a robust red with a certain charm in its straightforward fruity flavors. But increasingly producers of Sangiovese are making reserve wines of greater depth of bouquet and flavor with the capacity to age gracefully.

In Romagna, too, trends favor Sauvignon, Chardonnay, the Pinots and Cabernet. But many producers are devoting major efforts to developing superior strains of Sangiovese and Albana, while building interest in such rare local wines as the DOC white Pagadebit and red Cagnina and Bosco Eliceo Fortana.

DOCG

1 Albana di Romagna

DOC

2 Bosco Eliceo
3 Cagnina di Romagna
4 Colli Bolognesi
5 Colli Bolognesi Classico Pignoletto
6 Colli di Faenza
7 Colli di Imola
8 Colli di Parma
9 Colli di Rimini
10 Colli di Scandiano e di Canossa
11 Colli Piacentini
12 Lambrusco di Sorbara
13 Lambrusco Grasparossa di Castelvetro
14 Lambrusco Salamino di Santa Croce
15 Pagadebit di Romagna
16 Reggiano
17 Reno
18 Romagna Albana Spumante
19 Sangiovese di Romagna
20 Trebbiano di Romagna

DOCG (1)

Albana di Romagna : Secco W-Dr; Amabile or Dolce W-Sw; Passito W-Sw

DOC (19)

Bosco Eliceo : Bianco W-Dr/Sw/Fz; Fortana R-Dr/Sw/Fz; Merlot R-Dr; Sauvignon W-Dr/Sw/Fz

Cagnina di Romagna : R-Dr

Colli Bolognesi (Colline di Oliveto, Colline di Riosto, Colline Marconiane, Monte San Pietro, Serravalle, Zola Predosa) : Bianco W-Dr/Fz; Barbera R-Dr/Fz, Rs Ag-3; Cabernet Sauvignon R-Dr,

Rs Ag-3; Chardonnay W-Dr/Fz/Sp; Merlot R-Dr; Pignoletto W-Dr/Fz/Sp, also Sup; Pinot Bianco W-Dr/Fz/Sp; Sauvignon W-Dr/Fz, also Sup. (Each of the 6 subzones qualifies certain varietal wines with specific requirements under its appellation)

Colli Bolognesi Classico Pignoletto : W-Dr

Colli di Faenza : Bianco W-Dr; Rosso R-Dr, Rs Ag-2; Pinot Bianco W-Dr; Sangiovese R-Dr, Rs Ag-2; Trebbiano W-Dr

Colli di Imola : Bianco W-Dr/Fz, also Sup; Rosso R-Dr, Rs Ag-1.5, also Novello; Barbera R-Dr/Fz; Cabernet Sauvignon R-Dr. Rs Ag-1.5; Chardonnay W-Dr/Fz; Pignoletto W-Dr/Fz; Sangiovese R-Dr, Rs Ag-1.5; Trebbiano W-Dr/Fz

Colli di Parma : Rosso R-Dr; Malvasia W-Dr/Sw/Sp; Sauvignon W-Dr/Sp

Colli di Rimini : Bianco W-Dr; Rosso R-Dr; Biancame W-Dr; Cabernet Sauvignon R-Dr, Rs Ag-2; Rebola W-Dr/Sw; Rebola Passito W-Sw

Colli di Scandiano e di Canossa : Bianco W-Dr/Fz/Sp; Bianco Classico W-Dr/Fz; Cabernet Sauvignon R-Dr, Rs Ag-2; Chardonnay W-Dr/Fz/Sp; Lambrusco Grasparossa R-Dr/Fz; Lambrusco Montericco R-Dr/Fz; Malbo Gentile R-Dr/Fz, also Novello; Malvasia W-Dr/Sw/Fz/Sp; Marzemino R-Dr/Fz; Pinot W-Dr/Fz/Sp; Sauvignon W-Dr/Fz; Sauvignon Passito W-Sw

Colli Piacentini (Gutturnio, Monterosso Val d'Arda, Trebbianino Val Trebbia) : Gutturnio R-Dr/Fz, Sup Ag-1, Rs Ag-2; Gutturnio Classico R-Dr, Sup Ag-1, Rs Ag-2; Monterosso Val d'Arda W-Dr/Sw/Fz/Sp; Trebbianino Val Trebbia W-Dr/Sw/Fz/Sp; Val Nure W-Dr/Sw/Fz/Sp; Novello R-Dr; Vin Santo W-Sw Ag-4; Vin Santo di Vigoleno W/Sw Ag-5; Barbera R-Dr/Fz; Bonarda R-Dr/Sw/Fz/Sp; Cabernet Sauvignon R-Dr; Chardonnay W-Dr/Fz/Sp; Malvasia W-

Dr/Sw/Fz/Sp; Malvasia Passito W-Sw Ag-1; Ortrugo W-Dr/Sw/Fz/Sp; Pinot Grigio W-Dr/Fz/Sp; Pinot Nero R/P/W-Dr/Fz/Sp; Pinot Spumante W/P-Dr-Sp; Sauvignon W-Dr/Fz

Lambrusco di Sorbara : R/P-Fz/Dr/Sw

Lambrusco Grasparossa di Castelvetro : R/P-Fz/Dr/Sw

Lambrusco Salamino di Santa Croce : R/P-Fz/Dr/Sw

Pagadebit di Romagna (Bertinoro) : Secco W-Dr/Fz; Amabile W-Sw/Fz; Bertinoro Secco W-Dr/Fz, Amabile W-Sw/Fz

Reggiano : Bianco Spumante W-Dr-Sp; Rosso R-Dr/Fz, also Novello; Lambrusco R/P-Fz/Dr/Sw, also Novello; Lambrusco Salamino R/P-Fz/Dr/Sw

Reno : Bianco W-Dr/Sw/Fz; Montuni W-Dr/Sw/Fz; Pignoletto W-Dr/Sw/Fz

Romagna Albana Spumante : W-Sp-Dr/Sw

Sangiovese di Romagna : R-Dr, Rs Ag-2, also Novello

Trebbiano di Romagna : W-Dr/Fz/Sp

IGT (10)

Bianco di Castelfranco Emilia
Emilia or dell'Emilia
Fontana del Taro
Forlì
Modena or Provincia di Modena
Ravenna
Rubicone
Sillaro or Bianco di Sillaro
Terre di Veleja
Val Tidone

Liguria

Genoa (Genova) is the administrative center of Liguria, whose provinces include Imperia, La Spezia and Savona. The region ranks 18th in size (5,421 square kilometers) and 11th in population (1,633,000).

Vineyards cover 5,500 hectares, of which registered DOC plots total 750 hectares.

Annual wine production of 160,000 hectoliters (19th) includes 13% DOC, of which about 80% is white.

The rugged terrain of this slender seaside region makes grape growing a challenge, meaning that vineyards are scattered along the Italian Riviera and wine production is limited. Still some of the wines of Genoa's region, if hard to get to, are well worth the search.

The legend among Liguria's wines is Cinque Terre, a white made around the "five lands," a series of fishing villages nestled in the cliffs along the coast north of La Spezia. Vines there have been planted since antiquity on scarcely accessible terraces, some close enough to the Ligurian Sea to catch the spray from breaking waves. Most Cinque Terre is dry, though the sweet Sciacchetrà is coveted by those in the know.

Near La Spezia and crossing the border of Tuscany is the DOC zone of Colli di Luni where red and white wines, notably Vermentino, show class. The recent DOCs for Colline di Levanto and Golfo del Tigullio cover most of the other vineyards along the Riviera Levante, the coast to the southeast of Genoa, though some wines are still scarcely known beyond their localities.

Most of Liguria's limited commercial wine production is concentrated along the Ponente coast to the southwest. The first wine to be classified was Rossese di Dolceacqua, whose soft fruit and full flavor make it an uncommonly attractive red. The extensive Riviera Ligure di Ponente DOC zone covers the other classic wines of the area: the white Pigato and Vermentino and the red Ormeasco (a local Dolcetto) and Rossese.

Within the DOC zone are areas with special subdenominations for certain wines: Albenga and Finale for Pigato, Rossese and Vermentino and Riviera dei Fiori for all types. Like Vermentino, Pigato is a white of undeniable class whose prospects seem limited only by lack of vineyard space.

Most other wines of Liguria are curiosities, local whites and reds that are usually at their best young and close to home. Such rarities as Buzzeto and Granaccia, Coronata and Lumassina are uniquely and proudly Ligurian.

IGT (8)

Cinque Terre (Costa de Sera, Costa de Campu, Costa da Posa) : W-Dr

Cinque Terre Sciacchetrà : W-Sw Ag-1, Rs Ag-3

Colli di Luni (shared with Tuscany) : Bianco W-Dr; Rosso R-Dr, Rs Ag-2; Vermentino W-Dr

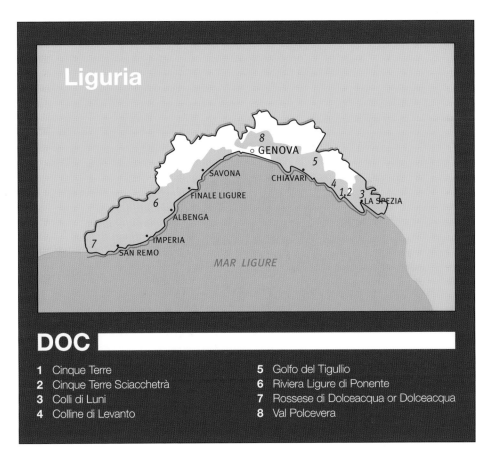

Liguria

° GENOVA

SAVONA
CHIAVARI
FINALE LIGURE
ALBENGA
IMPERIA
SAN REMO
LA SPEZIA

MAR LIGURE

DOC

1 Cinque Terre
2 Cinque Terre Sciacchetrà
3 Colli di Luni
4 Colline di Levanto

5 Golfo del Tigullio
6 Riviera Ligure di Ponente
7 Rossese di Dolceacqua or Dolceacqua
8 Val Polcevera

Colline di Levanto : Bianco W-Dr; Rosso R-Dr, also Novello

Golfo del Tigullio : Bianco W-Dr/Fz; Rosato P-Dr/Fz; Rosso R-Dr/Fz, also Novello; Spumante W-Dr-Sp; Passito W-Sw Ag-1; Bianchetta Genovese W-Dr/Fz; Ciliegiolo R-Dr/Fz, also Novello; Moscato W-Sw; Moscato Passito W-Sw Ag-1; Vermentino W-Dr/Fz

Riviera Ligure di Ponente (Albenga, Finale, Riviera dei Fiori) : *Ormeasco R-Dr, Sup Ag-1; *Ormeasco Siac-trà P-Sw; Pigato W-Dr; Rossese R-Dr; Vermentino W-Dr (*Ormeasco is made only in the Riviera dei Fiori subzone, other varietals are made in all 3)

Rossese di Dolceacqua or Dolceacqua : R-Dr, Sup Ag-1

Val Polcevera
Bianco W-Dr/Fz; Rosato P-Dr/Fz; Rosso R-Dr/Fz, also Novello; Passito W-Sw; Spumante W-Dr-Sp; Bianchetta W-Dr/Fz; Coronata W-Dr; Vermentino W-Dr/Fz

IGT (1)

Colline Savonesi

Lombardy (Lombardia)

Milan (Milano) is the administrative center of Lombardy, whose provinces include Bergamo, Brescia, Como, Cremona, Lecco, Lodi, Mantova, Pavia, Sondrio and Varese. The region ranks 4th in size (23,861 square kilometers) and 1st in population (9,029,000).

Vineyards cover 26,330 hectares, of which registered DOC or DOCG plots total 17,000 hectares.

Average annual wine production of 1,430,000 hectoliters (11th) includes about 50% of DOC or DOCG, of which more than 60% is red.

Wine does not rank high on the list of Lombardy's numerous industries. The citizens of this most populous and well-to-do region are better noted as consumers than producers of wine. Still, even though output is much less than that of neighboring Veneto, Emilia-Romagna and Piedmont, Lombardians do make some fine wine, a growing share of which is truly excellent.

Just why the inhabitants—the eclectic Milanese, in particular—downplay local wines is hard to explain. But regional wines are often upstaged on restaurant lists by the reds of Tuscany and Piedmont and the whites of the Venezie (Veneto, Trentino and Friuli). Many of the 6 million bottles of Nebbiolo reds produced annually in the Alpine Valtellina are spirited away by the neighboring Swiss before Italians have a chance at them.

On the other hand, Lombardians do show growing signs of pride in their preferences for the metodo classico sparkling wines of Franciacorta, which have attained the status of DOCG (while the red and white wines of the zone come under the Terre di Franciacorta DOC).

Lombardy boasts some highly favorable places for vines in a region where the Alpine climate is tempered by the lakes of Garda, Iseo, Como and Maggiore in the north, and the Apennines to the south.

The region's most productive zone, Oltrepò Pavese, also ranks as the most exploited. Much of its red and white wines are taken away in bulk or anonymous bottles to restaurants in Milan, Genoa and other cities. Oltrepò is Italy's leading source of Pinot Nero grapes, though growers let much of the supply slip away to Piedmontese and other bottlers of spumante, who issue the wines with little regard for origins.

Only a fraction of the wine produced annually in Oltrepò Pavese is sold as DOC—and then often at low prices. Unjustifiably, for some very good wines are made there, not only Pinots but robust Barbera, Bonarda and Oltrepò Pavese Rosso, plus fruity white Rieslings and Moscatos. Signs of a revival have been noted in local sparkling wines by both classical and tank methods of fermentation.

The Valtellina earns more respect abroad, and not only in Switzerland. DOCG has been granted to Valtellina Superiore and its four subdistricts: Grumello, Inferno, Sassella and Valgella. Those wines have gained favor in Italy and abroad, along with a bit of the rich and mellow Sfursat or Sforzato, which is included in the Valtellina DOC. The Superiore reds of Valtellina are among the most austere of Nebbiolos, due to the coolness of the terraced mountain vineyards, so steep in places that grapes are hauled in with baskets on cables. But the apparent lightness is deceptive, for some have the strength and stamina to improve for well over a decade.

Good wines are made in the provinces of Bergamo, Mantova and even Milano, but the prize for quality and variety goes to Brescia, which boasts a majority of the region's DOC/DOCGs: Botticino, Capriano del Colle, Cellatica, Franciacorta, Terre di Franciacorta, Garda Bresciano and three zones that share territory with Veneto: Garda, Lugana and San Martino della Battaglia. Under Garda DOC are four wines from the Garda Classico area in the province of Brescia. The white Lugana, which can compare with fine Soave Classico in class, has been growing in stature.

Lombardy's most admired wines of the moment are from Franciacorta. Terre di Franciacorta DOC applies to a sturdy red from Cabernet, Barbera and Nebbiolo, as well as to white wines from Pinot Bianco and Chardonnay. But Franciacorta's reputation has been built on the outstanding bottle-fermented sparkling wines fashioned by estates. Nearly a third of Italy's bottle-fermented sparkling wine is produced in the Brescia area, but only wines from select vineyards in the zone qualify as Franciacorta DOCG.

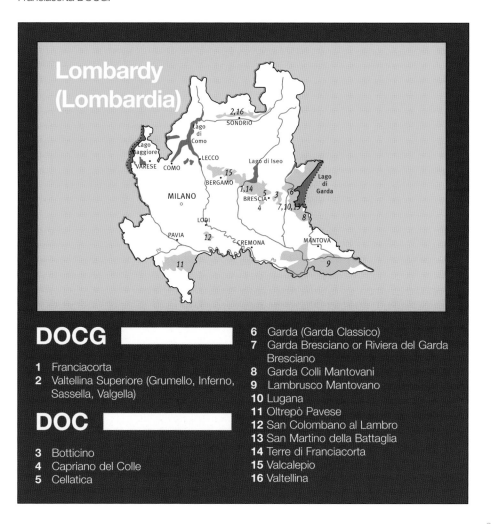

DOCG

1 Franciacorta
2 Valtellina Superiore (Grumello, Inferno, Sassella, Valgella)

DOC

3 Botticino
4 Capriano del Colle
5 Cellatica

6 Garda (Garda Classico)
7 Garda Bresciano or Riviera del Garda Bresciano
8 Garda Colli Mantovani
9 Lambrusco Mantovano
10 Lugana
11 Oltrepò Pavese
12 San Colombano al Lambro
13 San Martino della Battaglia
14 Terre di Franciacorta
15 Valcalepio
16 Valtellina

DOCG (2)

Franciacorta : W-Dr-Sp Ag2, Millesimato Ag-3, also Crémant or Satèn; Rosé P-Dr-Sp Ag2, Millesimato Ag-3

Valtellina Superiore (Grumello, Inferno, Sassella, Valgella) : R-Dr Ag-2, Rs Ag-3; Grumello or Inferno or Sassella or Valgella R-Dr Ag-2, Rs Ag-3

DOC (14)

Botticino : R-DR, Rs Ag-2

Capriano del Colle : Bianco or Trebbiano W-Dr/Fz; Rosso R-Dr, Rs Ag-2, also Novello

Cellatica : R-Dr, Sup Ag-1

Garda (shared with Veneto; Garda Classico is in Lombardy) : Garda Classico Bianco W-Dr; Garda Classico Chiaretto P-Dr; Garda Classico Groppello R-Dr, Rs Ag-2; Garda Classico Rosso R-Dr, Sup Ag-1; Frizzante W-Dr-Fz; Rosé P-Dr; Barbera R-Dr/Fz; Cabernet R-Dr; Cabernet Sauvignon R-Dr; Chardonnay W-Dr/Sp; Cortese W-Dr; Corvina R-Dr; Garganega W-Dr; Marzemino R-Dr; Merlot R-Dr; Pinot Bianco W-Dr/Sp; Pinot Grigio W-Dr; Pinot Nero R-Dr; Riesling W-Dr/Sp; Riesling Italico W-Dr; Sauvignon W-Dr; Tocai W-Dr

Garda Bresciano or Riviera del Garda Bresciano : Bianco W-Dr, Sup Ag-1; Chiaretto P-Dr, Sup Ag-1; Rosso R-Dr, Sup Ag-1, also Novello; Spumante Rosato P-Dr-Sp; Groppello R-Dr

Garda Colli Mantovani : Bianco W-Dr; Rosso R-Dr; Cabernet R-Dr, Rs Ag-2; Chardonnay W-Dr; Merlot R-Dr, Rs Ag-2; Pinot Bianco W-Dr; Pinot Grigio W-Dr; Sauvignon W-Dr; Tocai Italico W-Dr

Lambrusco Mantovano : Rosato P-Dr-Fz; Rosso R-Dr-Fz; Oltrepò Mantovano P/R-Dr-Fz; Viadanese-Sabbionetano P/R-Dr-Fz

Lugana (shared with Veneto) : W-DR, Sup Ag-1; Spumante W-Dr-Sp

Oltrepò Pavese : Rosato P-Dr/Fz; Rosso R-Dr/Fz, Rs Ag-2; Spumante Bianco W-Dr-Sp Ag-1.5, Millesimato Ag-2; Spumante Rosato P-Dr-Sp Ag-1.5, Millesimato Ag-2; Barbera R-Dr/Fz; Bonarda R-Dr/Sw/Fz; Buttafuoco R-Dr/Fz; Cabernet Sauvignon R-Dr; Chardonnay W-Dr/Fz/Sp; Cortese W-Dr/Fz/Sp; Malvasia W-Dr/Sw/Fz/Sp; Moscato W-Sw/Fz/Sp; Pinot Grigio W-Dr/Fz/Sp; Pinot Nero R/P/W-Dr/Fz; Pinot Nero Spumante R/P/W-Dr/Fz Ag-1.5, Millesimato Ag-2; Riesling Italico W-Dr/Fz; Riesling Renano W-DrSp; Sangue di Giuda R-Dr/Sw/Fz; Sauvignon W-Dr/Sp

San Colombano al Lambro : R-Dr

San Martino della Battaglia (shared with Veneto) : W-Dr; Liquoroso W-Sw-Ft

Terre di Franciacorta : Bianco W-Dr, Vigna Ag-1; Rosso R-Dr, Vigna Ag-2

Valcalepio : Bianco W-Dr; Rosso R-Dr Ag-1, Rs Ag-3; Moscato Passito W-Sw Ag-1.5; Moscato di Scanzo W-Sw Ag-1.5

Valtellina : R-Dr; Sfurzat or Sforzato R-Dr Ag-2

IGT (12)

Alto Mincio
Benaco Bresciano
Bergamasca
Collina del Milanese
Mantova or Provincia di Mantova
Montenetto di Brescia
Pavia or Provincia di Pavia
Quistello
Ronchi di Brescia
Sabbioneta
Sebino
Terrazze Retiche di Sondrio.

Piedmont (Piemonte)

Turin (Torino) is the administrative center of Piedmont, whose provinces include Alessandria, Asti, Biella, Cuneo, Novara, Torino, Verbano-Cusio-Ossola and Vercelli. The region ranks 2nd in size (25,399 square kilometers) and 5th in population (4,288,000).

Vineyards cover about 59,000 hectares, of which registered DOC or DOCG plots total 43,700 hectares (the most of any region).

Average annual wine production of 3,100,000 hectoliters (7th) includes more than 80% DOC or DOCG, of which about 65% is red.

Piedmont is admired above all for its red wines, led by the regal Barolo and Barbaresco. But the best known of the region's wines is the white, sweet, bubbly and widely adored Asti.

An overwhelming majority of Piedmont's wines derives from native vines. Besides the noble Nebbiolo—source of Barolo, Barbaresco, Gattinara and Ghemme, which are all DOCG—Barbera ranks as the most popular vine for reds, followed by Dolcetto, which is enjoyed for its mellow, round flavors. Brachetto makes sweet, fragrant bubbly red that is DOCG as Brachetto d'Acqui. Freisa and Grignolino lead a host of local varieties in rounding out the honor roll of reds.

Still, among classified wines, whites represent about a third of the volume. First comes Asti, whose DOCG applies to both sparkling Spumante and the softly bubbly Moscato d'Asti. With an average annual output of nearly 60 million liters, the Asti appellation ranks second in volume to Chianti among Italy's classified wines. An established star is Gavi, a dry white made from the native Cortese grape and a recent addition to the DOCG list.

Piedmont, Italy's westernmost region with borders on Switzerland and France, is hemmed in by the Alps and the Apennines, which explain why its name means "foot of the mountain." Though it ranks only seventh among the regions in total production, Piedmont is considered a giant of Italian wine in every other way.

Piedmont has the most DOC-DOCG zones with 50 and stands proud as the region with the largest percentage of its wines officially classified. It has no IGT. For craftsmanship, respect for tradition and devotion to native vines in their historical habitats, the Piedmontese have no rivals in Italy.

The climate is rigid by Italian standards, with distinct changes of season. Winters are cold with plenty of snow. Summers are for the most part hot and dry. Spring and fall are temperate to cool with fog normal at harvest time.

A majority of the region's vineyards are located in the Langhe and Monferrato hills, which are connected to the Apennines in the southeast. But several wines of significance are also grown along the foothills of the Alps to the north between Lake Maggiore and Valle d'Aosta.

The focal point of premium production is the town of Alba on the Tanaro River. In the nearby Langhe hills, Barolo ("king of wines and wine of kings") is produced at the rate of about 6 million bottles a year and Barbaresco, which many experts rate its equal, rarely reaches 2.5 million bottles. Both come from Nebbiolo, which gives them the powerful structure that makes them capable of improving for many years from such fine vintages as 2000 1999 1998 1997, 1996, 1990, 1989, 1985 and 1982.

DOCG

1 Asti (Moscato d'Asti)
2 Barbaresco
3 Barolo
4 Brachetto d'Acqui
5 Gattinara
6 Gavi or Cortese di Gavi
7 Ghemme

DOC

8 Albugnano
9 Barbera d'Alba
10 Barbera d'Asti
11 Barbera del Monferrato
12 Boca
13 Bramaterra
14 Canavese
15 Carema
16 Colli Tortonesi
17 Colline Novaresi
18 Colline Saluzzesi
19 Colline Torinesi
20 Cortese dell'Alto Monferrato
21 Coste della Sesia
22 Dolcetto d'Acqui
23 Dolcetto d'Alba
24 Dolcetto d'Asti
25 Dolcetto delle Langhe Monregalesi
26 Dolcetto di Diano d'Alba
27 Dolcetto di Dogliani
28 Dolcetto di Ovada
29 Erbaluce di Caluso
30 Fara
31 Freisa d'Asti
32 Freisa di Chieri
33 Gabiano
34 Grignolino d'Asti
35 Grignolino del Monferrato Casalese
36 Langhe

37 Lessona
38 Loazzolo
39 Malvasia di Casorzo d'Asti
40 Malvasia di Castelnuovo Don Bosco
41 Monferrato (Casalese)
42 Nebbiolo d'Alba
43 Piemonte*
44 Pinerolese
45 Roero (Arneis)
46 Rubino di Cantavenna
47 Ruchè di Castagnole Monferrato
48 Sizzano
49 Valsusa
50 Verduno Pelaverga o Verduno

*Wines may be produced throughout
 the region

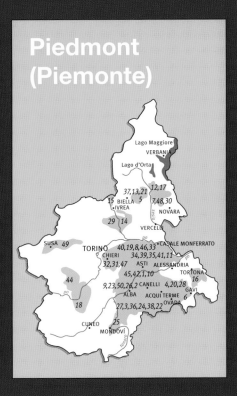

Piedmont (Piemonte)

The traditional Barolo and Barbaresco were admired almost as cult wines, though often criticized as too elaborate for modern palates. But the combination of favorable vintages and perfection of techniques among winemakers, many of them young, seems to be changing the old-fashioned image. Barolo and Barbaresco have retained their ample dimensions while becoming better balanced and more approachable than before.

The Alba area is renowned for its smooth, supple Dolcetto under several appellations, and for first-rate Nebbiolo and white Arneis from the Roero hills. But the most dramatic progress in the Alba and Asti areas has come with the ubiquitous Barbera, which after ages of being considered rather common has rapidly taken on aristocratic airs.

Certain aged Barberas have emerged to stand comparison with fine Nebbiolo reds. Piedmontese drink more red wine than white, and about half of the red is Barbera, which can also be attractive in youthfully fruity and bubbly versions. Three other red wines that have recovered after decades of decline are the crimson Grignolino, the often fizzy Freisa and the buoyantly sweet and bubbly Brachetto from Acqui.

In the other major area of Nebbiolo production, the hills to the north, modern styles are emerging in such reds as Carema, Lessona, Sizzano, Fara and the long vaunted Gattinara, which along with neighboring Ghemme has been granted DOCG.

Piedmont is a leading producer of sparkling wines. Foremost among them is Asti, the world's most popular sweet bubbly wine. The market for this fragrant white is actually larger abroad than in Italy. In fact, worldwide demand is so great that a shortage of Moscato di Canelli grapes has developed. Piedmont is also a major producer of dry sparkling wines by both the classical and charmat methods, though many of the Chardonnay and Pinot grapes used for them originate outside the region, mainly in neighboring Oltrepò Pavese in Lombardy or in Trentino-Alto Adige.

Among still whites, Gavi shows a crisp yet elegant style that explains why admirers consider it one of the best with seafood and why it was recently promoted to DOCG. Smoothly fruity Arneis continues to gain ground in Roero, where the light, zesty Favorita is also emerging. Some predict a revival of the ancient white Erbaluce di Caluso from near Turin.

Although Piedmontese growers were among the first to experiment with such foreign varieties as Cabernet and the Pinots early in the19th century, those vines had largely faded from favor. Just recently, though, Cabernet Sauvignon, Pinot Bianco and Nero and, especially, Chardonnay have shown promise. The regional Piemonte DOC applies in part to sparkling wines from Chardonnay, Pinots and other varieties. Still, as admirers have noted, even wines from international varieties bear a stamp that is unmistakably Piedmontese.

DOCG (7)

Asti : Asti or Asti Spumante W-Sw-Sp; Moscato d'Asti W-Sw-Fz

Barbaresco : R-Dr Ag-2, Rs Ag-4

Barolo : R-Dr Ag-3, Rs Ag-5

Brachetto d'Acqui : R-Sw-Fz; Spumante R-Sw-Sp

Gattinara : R-Dr Ag-3, Rs Ag-4

Gavi or Cortese di Gavi : W-Dr/Fz/Sp

Ghemme : R-Dr Ag-3, Rs Ag-4

DOC (43)

Albugnano : R-Dr, Sup Ag-1; Rosato P-Dr

Barbera d'Alba : R-Dr, Sup Ag-1

Barbera d'Asti : R-Dr, Sup Ag-1

Barbera del Monferrato : R-Dr, Sup Ag-1

Boca : R-Dr Ag-3

Bramaterra : R-Dr Ag-2, Rs Ag-3

Canavese : Bianco W-Dr; Rosato P-Dr; Rosso R-Dr, also Novello; Barbera R-Dr; Nebbiolo R-Dr

Carema : R-Dr Ag-3, Rs Ag-4

Colli Tortonesi : Bianco W-Dr; Chiaretto P-Dr; Rosso R-Dr, also Novello; Barbera R-Dr, Sup Ag-1; Cortese W-Dr/SwFz/Sp; Dolcetto R-Dr, also Novello

Colline Novaresi : Bianco W-Dr; Barbera R-Dr, also Novello; Bonarda or Uva Rara R-Dr, also Novello; Croatina R-Dr, also Novello; Nebbiolo or Spanna R-Dr, also Novello; Vespolina R-Dr, also Novello

Colline Saluzzesi : R-Dr; Pelaverga R-Dr; Quagliano R-Sw/Sp

Colline Torinesi : Rosso R-Dr, also Novello; Barbera R-Dr; Bonarda R-Dr/Sw; Malvasia R-Sw/Fz; Pelaverga R-Dr

Cortese dell'Alto Monferrato : W-Dr/Fz/Sp

Coste della Sesia : Bianco W-Dr; Rosato P-Dr; Rosso R-Dr, also Novello; Bonarda R-Dr; Croatina R-Dr; Nebbiolo or Spanna R-Dr; Vespolina R-Dr

Dolcetto d'Acqui : R-Dr, Sup Ag-1

Dolcetto d'Alba : R-Dr, Sup Ag-1

Dolcetto d'Asti : R-Dr, Sup Ag-1

Dolcetto delle Langhe Monregalesi : R-Dr, Sup Ag-1

Dolcetto di Diano d'Alba or Diano d'Alba : R-Dr, Sup Ag-1

Dolcetto di Dogliani : R-Dr, Sup Ag-1

Dolcetto di Ovada : R-Dr, Sup Ag-1

Erbaluce di Caluso : W-Dr; Spumante W-Dr-Sp; Passito W-Sw Ag4, Rs Ag-5

Fara : R-Dr Ag-3

Freisa d'Asti : R-Dr/Sw/Fz/Sp, Sup Ag-1

Freisa di Chieri : R-Dr/Sw/Fz/Sp, Sup Ag-1

Gabiano : R-Dr, Rs Ag-2

Grignolino d'Asti : R-Dr

Grignolino del Monferrato Casalese : R-Dr

Langhe : Bianco W-Dr; Rosso R-Dr; Arneis W-Dr; Chardonnay W-Dr, also Vigna; Dolcetto R-Dr; Favorita W-Dr, also Vigna; Freisa R-Dr/Fz, also Vigna; Nebbiolo R-Dr

Lessona : R-Dr Ag-2

Loazzolo : W-Sw Ag-2, Vendemmia Tardiva W-Sw Ag-2

Malvasia di Casorzo d'Asti : P/R/Sw/Fz; Passito R-Sw; Spumante P-Sw-Sp

Malvasia di Castelnuovo Don Bosco : R/Sw/Fz; Spumante R-Sw-Sp

Monferrato (Casalese) : Bianco W-Dr; Chiaretto or Ciaret P-Dr, also Novello; Rosso R-Dr, also Novello; Monferrato Casalese Cortese W-Dr; Dolcetto R-Dr, also Novello; Freisa R-Dr/Fz, also Novello

Nebbiolo d'Alba : Secco R-Dr Ag-1; Spumante R-Sw-Sp

Piemonte : Spumante W-Dr-Sp; Barbera R-Dr, also Novello; Bonarda R-Dr/Sw, also Novello; Brachetto R-Sw/Fz, also Novello; Chardonnay W-Dr/Sp; Chardonnay-Pinot Spumante W-Dr-Sp; Cortese W-Dr/Sp; Grignolino R-Dr, also Novello; Moscato W-Sw/Fz; Moscato Passito W/Sw Ag-1; Pinot Bianco Spumante W-Dr-Sp; Pinot Grigio Spumante W-Dr-Sp; Pinot Nero Spumante W-Dr-Sp; Pinot Spumante W-Dr-Sp; Pinot-Chardonnay Spumante W-Dr-Sp

Pinerolese : Rosato P-Dr; Rosso R-Dr; Barbera R-Dr; Bonarda R-Dr/Sw; Dolcetto R-Dr; Doux d'Henry R-Dr; Freisa R-Dr/Fz; Ramie R-Dr

Roero : R-Dr, also Sup; Arneis W-Dr/Sp

Rubino di Cantavenna : R-Dr Ag-1

Ruchè di Castagnole Monferrato : R-Dr

Sizzano : R-Dr Ag-3

Valsusa : R-Dr

Verduno Pelaverga or Verduno : R-Dr

Valle d'Aosta

This tiniest of regions, tucked into Italy's mountainous north-western corner against the borders of Switzerland and France, has precious little space for vines on its rocky Alpine terraces. But the minuscule amounts of wine it does produce are distinct from anything else in Italy or its foreign neighbors.

A regionwide DOC known as Valle d'Aosta or Vallée d'Aoste covers 23 categories of wine whose names are given in Italian and French, the official second language. These include the longstanding DOCs of Donnas and Enfer d'Arvier, as well as the white wines of Morgex and La Salle, whose vineyards in the shadow of Mont Blanc are reputed to be the highest in continental Europe. Valle d'Aosta has no IGT. But whether Valle d'Aosta's wines are classified or not, they could never be more than curios that are most compelling when drunk on the spot.

Grape varieties range from Piedmontese (Nebbiolo, Dolcetto, Moscato) to French (Chardonnay, the Pinots, Gamay), to the teutonic Muller Thurgau called in for mountain duty. But the most intriguing wines of Valle d'Aosta stem from varieties it calls its own. These include the Petit Rouge of Enfer d'Arvier and Torrette, the Blanc de Valdigne of Morgex and La Salle, the Petite Arvine of the varietal white of the name, the Vien for the red wine of Nus and the Malvoisie (apparently a mutation of Pinot Gris) for the rare dessert white of Nus.

Six cooperative wineries with 450 growers account for about three-quarters of Valle D'Aosta's wine and are largely responsible for a steady improvement in quality.

Aosta is the administrative center and lone province of Valle d'Aosta, which ranks 20th among the regions in both size (3,264 square kilometers) and population (120,000).

Vineyards cover 650 hectares, of which registered DOC plots total 156 hectares.

Average annual wine production of 31,000 hectoliters (20th) includes about 20% DOC, of which more than 75% is red.

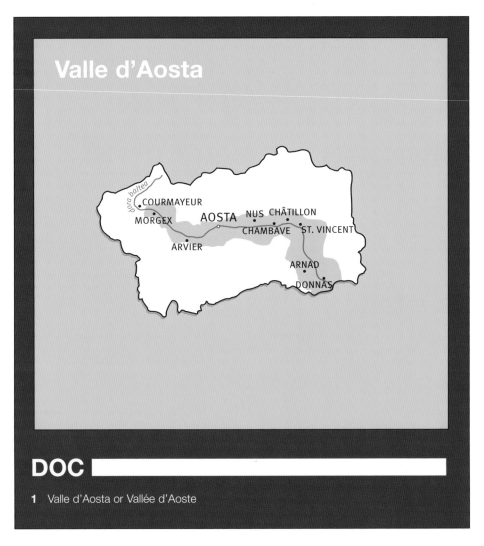

Valle d'Aosta

DOC

1 Valle d'Aosta or Vallée d'Aoste

DOC (1)

Valle d'Aosta or Vallée d'Aoste : Bianco/Blanc W-Dr/Fz; Rosato/Rosé P-Dr; Rosso/Rouge R-Dr, also Novello; Arnad Montjovet R-Dr, Sup Ag-1; Blanc de Morgex et de La Salle W-Dr/Fz; Chambave Moscato/Muscat W-Dr/Sw; Chambave Moscato Passito/Muscat Fletri W-Dr/Sw Ag-1; Chambave Rosso/Rouge R-Dr; Chardonnay W-Dr; Donnas R-Dr Ag-2; Enfer d'Arvier R-Dr; Fumin R-Dr; Gamay R-Dr; Müller Thurgau W-Dr; Nus Malvoisie W-Dr; Nus Malvoisie Passito W-Sw Ag-1; Nus Rosso/Rouge R-Dr; Petit Rouge R-Dr; Petite Arvine W-Dr; Pinot Grigio/Pinot Gris W-Dr; Pinot Nero/Pinot Noir R-Dr or W-Dr; Premetta R-Dr; Torrette R-Dr, also Sup

The Northeast: Taste of the Future in the Venezie

Veneto, Friuli-Venezia Giulia, Trentino-Alto Adige

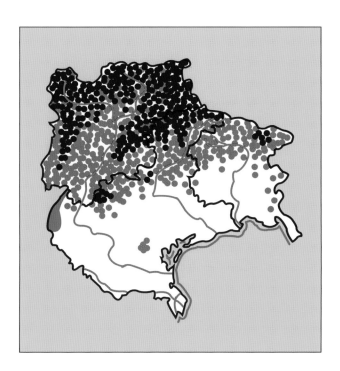

The three northeastern regions, known collectively as the Tre Venezie or simply the Venezie, set the pace in Italy in the crafting of modern wines from a great range of varieties both native and international. They began in the 1970s by introducing new techniques for production of white wines, following up in recent decades with ever more sophisticated methods for reds.

Two of Italy's leading wine schools are located in the Venezie (at San Michele all'Adige in Trentino and Conegliano in Veneto). The world's largest vine nursery is at Rauscedo in Friuli. The nation's most important wine fair, Vinitaly, is held each spring in Verona.

Together Veneto, Friuli-Venezia Giulia and Trentino-Alto Adige produce less than a fifth of Italy's total volume of wine but account for about a third of the DOC. Veneto leads the way, after recently replacing Apulia and Sicily as the largest producer of wine among the 20 regions, while increasing its leadership with DOC, due in great part to the Verona trio of Soave, Valpolicella and Bardolino. Friuli-Venezia Giulia and Trentino-Alto Adige are modest producers in terms of volume but boast enviable percentages of classified wines in the total.

The determining quality factor in all three regions is the climate influenced by the Alps, of which the Venezie are on the sunny side, protected from the damp cold of northern Europe. Vineyard conditions range from cool at high altitudes to warm near the shores of the Adriatic Sea and along the valleys of the Po, Adige, Piave and Tagliamento rivers.

Although the culture of the Venezie, like the name, was determined by the ancient Venetian Republic, strong influences can be felt from Austria and the Balkans. One result is a cosmopolitan mix of vine varieties. Growers here work with an amazing assortment of native and imported vines to produce what are indisputably a majority of Italy's fine white wines and a multitude of reds, ranging from the young and simplistic to the aged and complex.

In contemporary times, white wines led by Soave and Pinot Grigio had become popular around the world. But producers in Friuli and Trentino-Alto Adige have fashioned wines of depth and style to dispel the notion that Italian whites are by nature light and fresh. Recently the trend that had favored whites in the Venezie has started to reverse with increased plantings of varieties for red wines.

Verona's Soave, Valpolicella and Bardolino derive from native varieties. But in the central and eastern Veneto and Friuli imported varieties—such as Merlot, Cabernet, the Pinots, Chardonnay and Sauvignon—share vineyard space with the local Tocai, Prosecco, Verduzzo, Refosco, Schioppettino, Ribolla Gialla and Raboso.

In Trentino-Alto Adige red wines still prevail, dominated by the ubiquitous Schiava or Vernatsch, though the more distinguished Teroldego, Lagrein and Marzemino hold their own against Cabernet, Merlot and Pinot Nero. White varieties have gained prominence there, led by Chardonnay, the Pinots, Sauvignon and Gewürztraminer.

Since so many varieties are grown, the practice in all three regions has been to group wines under a single DOC name for a large geographical area, such as Veneto's Piave, Friuli's Collio Goriziano and the province-wide appellations of Trentino and Alto Adige. Though the lists may be long, this geographical identity seems to aid consumers in connecting places with types of wine.

Veneto

Venice's region has emerged in recent times as Italy's largest producer of wine with a major share classified as DOC or DOCG (more than 300 million bottles a year). Leading the flow is Verona's trio of Soave, Valpolicella and Bardolino. But since DOC represents less than a third of the region's total, the Veneto also figures as a major producer and exporter of IGT wines, often of moderate price.

The Veneto has three general areas of premium wine production: the western province of Verona in the hills between Lake Garda and the town of Soave; the central hills in the provinces of Vicenza, Padova and Treviso; the eastern plains of the Piave and Tagliamento river basins along the Adriatic coast northeast of Venice.

Verona's classic wines are bona fide natives. Soave, from Garganega and Trebbiano di Soave, is usually dry and still, though sparkling and sweet Recioto versions are also prescribed. Soave, the most popular of Italian dry whites, ranks third after Chianti and Asti in volume among classified wines (with more than 50 million liters a year).

Valpolicella, made from a blend of Corvina, Rondinella and Molinara grapes, has been fourth in volume among DOCs with more than 30 million liters. Valpolicella is noted as a hearty red to drink relatively young, though grapes from its vineyards in the hills north of Verona can also be partly dried and made into the richly dry Amarone della Valpolicella or the opulently sweet Recioto della Valpolicella.

Amarone, amply structured and long on the palate, ranks among Italy's most authoritative red wines with a list of admirers growing around the world. It is unquestionably one of the great red wines for aging.

Bardolino from the same basic grapes as Valpolicella, is enviably easy to drink, whether in the red Superiore which has recently become DOCG or the dark pink Chiaretto version. Bardolino has also gained in popularity as a Vino Novello, another category in which Veneto leads production in Italy. Bardolino, from the shores of Lake Garda, also ranks high in terms of volume with about 20 million liters a year.

Another Veronese DOC wine of note is Bianco di Custoza, a crisp white much appreciated in northern Italy. Verona also shares two DOCs with Lombardy: Lugana and Garda. A distinctive DOC produced between Verona and Vicenza is Lessini Durello, a steely dry white, usually sparkling, that seems destined for wider recognition. The Veronese also make alternative wines of distinction, especially the reds produced by the so-called ripasso method in which the basic Valpolicella is refermented with the pomace of Amarone to gain body and structure.

Venice (Venezia) is the administrative center of Veneto, whose provinces include Belluno, Padova, Rovigo, Treviso, Verona and Vicenza. The region ranks 8th in size (18,391 square kilometers) and 6th in population (4,488,000).

Vineyards cover 76,860 hectares, of which registered DOC or DOCG plots total 34,637 hectares.

Average annual wine production of 8,630,000 hectoliters (1st) includes about 30% DOC or DOCG, of which nearly 60% is white.

The Veneto's central hills take in several DOC zones. Near Vicenza are Gambellara, with whites similar to those of neighboring Soave, and Colli Berici, where varietal wines from Tocai, the Pinots, Merlot and Cabernet prevail. Also in the province is Breganze, where Cabernet, Merlot and whites from the Pinots and Chardonnay have earned a reputation, though the most admired wine is often the sweet Torcolato. Near Padova are the Colli Euganei range of hills, whose sheer slopes render a range of red and white varietals.

Treviso's province takes in the hills north of Venice between the towns of Conegliano and Valdobbiadene, noted for the popular Prosecco, a dry to softly sweet white, almost always bubbly. A refined version is known as Superiore di Cartizze. The adjacent Montello e Colli Asolani zone is noted for Prosecco, Cabernet and Merlot. Producers of Prosecco have used their experience with sparkling wine to build markets with Pinot and Chardonnay, made either by the tank fermentation or the classical bottle fermentation methods.

The plains northeast of Venice take in the Piave DOC zone, where Merlot and Cabernet dominate a large range of trendy varietals, though the local red Raboso and white Verduzzo still attract admirers. Lison-Pramaggiore (previously noted for white Tocai and Cabernet and Merlot) has a full list of popular varietals.

Merlot and Cabernet Franc have been the workhorse varieties of the central and eastern Veneto for decades, often in light and easy wines to drink young. But some producers blend the two, increasingly with Cabernet Sauvignon, and age the wines in small oak barrels to develop greater style and complexity.

Among white varieties, Pinot Grigio, Sauvignon and Chardonnay continue to gain ground, often in youthfully fruity versions but also as oak-aged wines of depth and style.

Veneto shares five DOC zones with other regions: Garda, Lugana and San Martino della Battaglia with Lombardy, Lison-Pramaggiore with Friuli-Venezia Giulia and Valdadige with Trentino-Alto Adige.

DOCG (2)

Bardolino Superiore (Classico) : R-Dr, Sup Ag-1, (Classico applies to wines from the original zone)

Recioto di Soave (Classico) : W-Sw Ag-1; Spumante W-Sw-Sp (Classico applies to wines from the original zone)

DOC (19)

Arcole : Bianco W-Dr/Sp; Rosso R-Dr, also Novello; Cabernet R-Dr, Rs Ag-2; Cabernet Sauvignon R-Dr, Rs Ag-2; Chardonnay W-Dr/Fz; Garganega W-Dr; Merlot R-Dr, Rs Ag-2; Pinot Bianco W-Dr; Pinot Grigio W-Dr

Bagnoli di Sopra or Bagnoli (Classico) : Bianco W-Dr; Rosato P-Dr; Rosso R-Dr, Rs Ag-2; Passito W-Sw Ag-2; Spumante W/P-Dr-Sp; Cabernet R-Dr, Rs Ag-2; Friularo R-Dr, Rs Ag-2; Merlot R-Dr, Rs Ag-2 (Classico applies to all wines but Passito and Spumante from the original zone; all wines may be qualified as Vigna)

Bardolino (Classico) : R-Dr, also Novello; Chiaretto P-Dr/Sp (Classico applies to wines from the original zone)

Bianco di Custoza : W-Dr/Sp

Breganze : Bianco W-Dr, also Sup; Rosato P-Dr; Rosso R-Dr, also Sup, Rs Ag-2; Cabernet R-Dr, also Sup, Rs Ag-2; Cabernet Sauvignon R-Dr, also Sup, Rs Ag-2; Chardonnay W-Dr, also Sup; Marzemino R-Dr, also Sup, Rs Ag-2; Pinot Bianco W-Dr, also Sup; Pinot Grigio W-Dr, also Sup; Pinot Nero R-Dr, also Sup, Rs Ag-2; Sauvignon W-Dr, also Sup; Torcolato W-Sw Ag-1, Rs Ag-2; Vespaiolo W-Dr, also Sup

Colli Berici : Spumante W-Dr-Sp; Cabernet R-Dr, Rs Ag-3; Chardonnay W-Dr; Garganega W-Dr; Merlot R-Dr; Pinot Bianco W-Dr; Sauvignon W-Dr; Tocai Italico W-Dr; Tocai Rosso R-Dr; Tocai Rosso di Barbarano or Barbarano R-Dr

Colli di Conegliano : Bianco W-Dr; Rosso R-Dr Ag-2; Refrontolo Passito R-Sw; Torchiato di Fregona W-Sw Ag-1

Colli Euganei : Bianco W-Dr; Bianco Spumante W-Dr-Sp; Rosso R-Dr, Rs Ag-2,

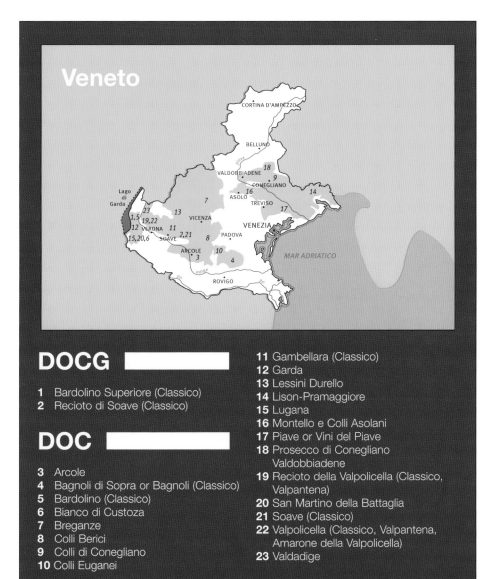

DOCG

1   Bardolino Superiore (Classico)
2   Recioto di Soave (Classico)

DOC

3   Arcole
4   Bagnoli di Sopra or Bagnoli (Classico)
5   Bardolino (Classico)
6   Bianco di Custoza
7   Breganze
8   Colli Berici
9   Colli di Conegliano
10 Colli Euganei

11 Gambellara (Classico)
12 Garda
13 Lessini Durello
14 Lison-Pramaggiore
15 Lugana
16 Montello e Colli Asolani
17 Piave or Vini del Piave
18 Prosecco di Conegliano
    Valdobbiadene
19 Recioto della Valpolicella (Classico,
    Valpantena)
20 San Martino della Battaglia
21 Soave (Classico)
22 Valpolicella (Classico, Valpantena,
    Amarone della Valpolicella)
23 Valdadige

also Novello; Cabernet R-Dr, Rs Ag-2; Cabernet Franc R-Dr, Rs Ag-2; Cabernet Sauvignon R-Dr, Rs Ag-2; Chardonnay W-Dr/Sp; Fior d'Arancio Passito W-Sw; Fior d'Arancio Spumante W-Sw-Sp; Merlot R-Dr, Rs Ag-2; Moscato W-Sw/Sp; Pinello W-Sw/Fz; Pinot Bianco W-Dr/Sp; Serprino W-Dr/Fz; Tocai Italico W-Dr

Gambellara (Classico) : W-Dr; Recioto W-Sw/Sp; Vin Santo W-Sw Ag-2 (Classico applies to wines from the original zone)

Garda (shared with Lombardy) : Frizzante W-Dr-Fz; Rosé P-Dr; Barbera R-Dr/Fz; Cabernet R-Dr; Cabernet Sauvignon R-Dr; Chardonnay W-Dr/Sp; Cortese W-Dr; Corvina R-Dr; Garganega W-Dr; Marzemino R-Dr; Merlot R-Dr; Pinot Bianco W-Dr/Sp; Pinot Grigio W-Dr; Pinot Nero R-Dr; Riesling W-Dr/Sp; Riesling Italico W-Dr; Sauvignon W-Dr; Tocai W-Dr (Classico applies to wines from the original zone in Lombardy)

Lessini Durello : W-Dr, also Sup; Spumante W-Dr Sp

Lison-Pramaggiore (shared with Friuli-Venezia Giulia) : Cabernet R-Dr/Sp, Rs Ag-3; Cabernet Franc R-Dr/Sp, Rs Ag-3; Cabernet Sauvignon R-Dr/Sp, Rs Ag-3; Chardonnay W-Dr/Sp; Refosco del Peduncolo Rosso R-Dr/Sp; Merlot R-Dr/Sp, Rs Ag-2; Pinot Bianco W-Dr/Sp; Pinot Grigio W-Dr/Sp; Riesling Italico W-Dr/Sp; Sauvignon W-Dr/Sp; Tocai Italico W-Dr/Sp; Tocai Italico Classico W-Dr/Sp; Verduzzo W-Dr/Sw/Sp (Classico applies to Tocai Italico from the original zone around Lison in Veneto)

Lugana (shared with Lombardy) : W-DR, Sup Ag-1; Spumante W-Dr-Sp

Montello e Colli Asolani : Rosso R-Dr, Sup Ag-2; Cabernet R-Dr, Sup Ag-2; Cabernet Franc R-Dr, Sup Ag-2; Cabernet Sauvignon R-Dr, Sup Ag-2; Chardonnay W-Dr/Sp; Merlot R-Dr, Sup Ag-2; Pinot Bianco W-Dr/Sp; Pinot Grigio W-Dr; Prosecco W-Dr/Sw/Fz; Prosecco Spumante W-Dr/Sw-Sp

Piave or Vini del Piave : Cabernet R-Dr, Rs Ag-3; Cabernet Sauvignon R-Dr, Rs Ag-3; Chardonnay W-Dr; Merlot R-Dr, Rs Ag-2; Pinot Bianco W-Dr; Pinot Grigio W-Dr; Pinot Nero R-Dr; Raboso R-Dr Ag-3; Tocai Italico W-Dr; Verduzzo W-Dr/Sw

Prosecco di Conegliano Valdobbiadene : W-Dr/Sw/Fz; Spumante W-Dr/Sw-Sp; Superiore di Cartizze W-Dr/Sw-Sp

Recioto della Valpolicella (Classico, Valpantena) : R-Sw; Spumante R-Sw-Sp (Classico applies to wines from the original zone; Valpantena to a sector of the territory)

San Martino della Battaglia (shared with Lombardy) : W-Dr; Liquoroso W-Sw-Ft

Soave (Classico) : W-Dr, also Sup; Spumante W-Dr-Sp (Classico applies to wines from the original zone)

Valpolicella (Classico, Valpantena, Amarone della Valpolicella) : R-Dr, Sup Ag-1; Amarone della Valpolicella R-Dr Ag-2 (Classico applies to wines from the original zone; Valpantena to a sector of the territory)

Valdadige : Bianco W-Dr; Rosato P-Dr; Rosso R-Dr; Chardonnay W-Dr; Pinot Grigio W-Dr; Pinot Bianco W-Dr; Schiava R-Dr

IGT (10)

Alto Livenza

Colli Trevigiani

Conselvano

Marca Trevigiana

Vallagarina

Veneto

Veneto Orientale

Veronese or Provincia di Verona

Venezie or delle Venezie

Vigneti delle Dolomiti

Friuli-Venezia Giulia

The compact region of Friuli-Venezia Giulia, commanding the northern Adriatic Sea with borders on Austria and Slovenia, continues to set the pace with modern Italian white wine. Drawing from worthy native varieties and the choicest of the international array, Friulians have applied studied vineyard techniques and avant-garde enology to the production of highly distinctive whites, as well as some eminently attractive reds.

Friuli has two DOC zones of exceptional status in Collio Goriziano, or simply Collio, and Colli Orientali del Friuli, adjacent areas that follow the border of Slovenia from Gorizia west and northwest to Tarcento. The exchange of air currents between the Alps and the Adriatic has created a highly favorable habitat for vines on the terraced slopes called ronchi. Carso is a unique zone in the hills above the seaport and regional capital of Trieste. The other six DOC zones cover low hills or plains, but quality there can be convincing, most notably from Isonzo, which rivals Collio and Colli Orientali for the class of certain wines.

Varietal wines dominate the multitude of types included in Friuli-Venezia Giulia's nine DOC categories (including part of Lison-Pramaggiore, shared with Veneto). Only the Friuli Grave zone is large by national standards, producing some 30 million liters a year to stand with the top ten DOCs in volume.

Friuli has built a glowing reputation in Italy and abroad for white wines made by relatively small wineries and estates. The whites had long been dominated by Tocai Friulano, a variety related to Sauvignon Vert or Sauvignonasse. But recently a European court ruled that Tocai must change its name so as not to be confused with the Tokay or Tokaji of Hungary, which is the name of a wine but not a vine.

Friuli's Malvasia Istriana, Ribolla Gialla and Verduzzo also can be intriguing, as can such admirable foreign varieties as Sauvignon, Chardonnay and Pinot Bianco and the ever popular Pinot Grigio.

The Friulian style in whites favors the exquisitely fresh and fruity, with delicate fragrance and flavor that express clear varietal character. Many producers consider their whites to be too pure and linear to benefit from wood aging. The style has been on target for the national market, which seems to favor the flavors and names of pure varietals. But there are a growing number of exceptions to the rule, in white wines that gain depth and complexity from blending, oak aging and other artistic touches.

Friulian reds were traditionally light and fruity, best to drink

Trieste is the administrative center of Friuli-Venezia Giulia, whose provinces include Gorizia, Pordenone and Udine. The region ranks 17th in size (7,855 square kilometers) and 15th in population (1,184,000).

Vineyards cover 18,550 hectares, of which registered DOC plots total 12,754 hectares.

Average annual wine production of 1,160,000 hectoliters (14th) includes 60% DOC, of which about 60% is white.

within two to five years of the harvest. That style applied to the predominant Merlot and Cabernet Franc, as well as to Pinot Nero and the worthy native variety of Refosco. But certain winemakers have heightened structure and nuance by blending Cabernet Sauvignon, Merlot and other varieties and aging the wine in small oak barrels.

Friulians have shown an encouraging tendency to revive varieties that had been neglected. Foremost among the legends is Picolit, a white that ranked as one of Europe's finest sweet wines around 1800, when it was favored by the Hapsburgs and other royal families. Despite low yields, Picolit has been coming back. So has Verduzzo, which makes refined dessert wines in a place called Ramandolo in the Colli Orientali. Ribolla Gialla, a native of Collio, has benefited from new methods that make it into a dry white of character.

Among the reds are Refosco, also known as Terrano, which can be made either light and fruity or into a durable wine for aging. Though rare and odd, Franconia and Tazzelenghe make distinctive reds, but perhaps the Pignolo and Schioppettino varieties have the most intriguing potential.

Sparkling wines represent a growing field, as producers bring not only choice Pinot and Chardonnay grapes into their cuvées but also Ribolla for fine spumante by the classical and charmat methods.

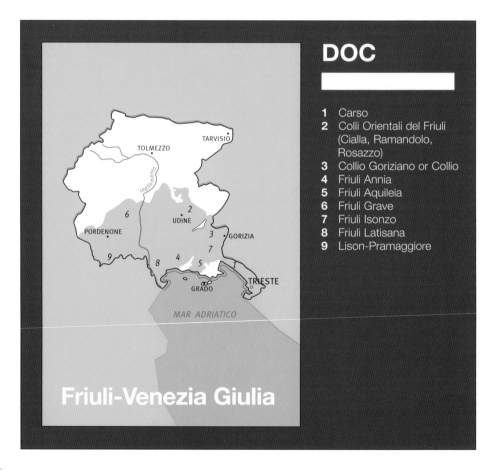

DOC

1 Carso
2 Colli Orientali del Friuli (Cialla, Ramandolo, Rosazzo)
3 Collio Goriziano or Collio
4 Friuli Annia
5 Friuli Aquileia
6 Friuli Grave
7 Friuli Isonzo
8 Friuli Latisana
9 Lison-Pramaggiore

Friuli-Venezia Giulia

Carso : Rosso R-Dr; Terrano R-Dr; Cabernet Franc R-Dr; Cabernet Sauvignon R-Dr; Chardonnay W-Dr; Malvasia W-Dr; Merlot R-Dr; Pinot Grigio W-Dr; Refosco R-Dr; Sauvignon W-Dr; Terrano R-Dr; Vitouska W-Dr

Colli Orientali del Friuli (Cialla, Ramandolo, Rosazzo) : Bianco W-Dr, Rs Ag-2; Rosato P-Dr, Rs Ag-2; Rosso R-Dr, Rs Ag-2; Cabernet R-Dr, Rs Ag-2; Cabernet Franc R-Dr, Rs Ag-2; Cabernet Sauvignon R-Dr, Rs Ag-2; Chardonnay W-Dr, Rs Ag-2; Malvasia W-Dr, Rs Ag-2; Merlot R-Dr, Rs Ag-2; Müller Thurgau W-Dr, Rs Ag-2; Picolit W-Sw, Rs Ag-2; Pignolo R-Dr, Rs Ag-2; Pinot Bianco W-Dr, Rs Ag-2; Pinot Grigio W-Dr, Rs Ag-2; Pinot Nero R-Dr, Rs Ag-2; Refosco R-Dr, Rs Ag-2; Ribolla Gialla W-Dr, Rs Ag-2; Riesling W-Dr, Rs Ag-2; Sauvignon W-Dr, Rs Ag-2; Schioppettino R-Dr, Rs Ag-2; Tazzelenghe R-Dr, Rs Ag-2; Tocai Friulano W-Dr, Rs Ag-2; Traminer Aromatico W-Dr, Rs Ag-2; Verduzzo Friulano W-Dr/Sw, Rs Ag-2 (All preceding wines have a Superiore version requiring lower vine yields and a higher degree of natural alcohol); Cialla: Bianco W-Dr, Rs Ag-4; Rosso R-Dr, Rs Ag-4; Picolit W-Sw Ag-2, Rs Ag-4; Refosco R-Dr Ag-2, Rs Ag-4; Ribolla Gialla W-Dr, Rs Ag-4; Schioppettino R-Dr Ag-2, Rs Ag-4; Verduzzo Friulano W-Sw Ag-2, Rs Ag-4; Ramandolo: W-Sw; Rosazzo: Bianco W-Dr, Rs Ag-2; Rosso R-Dr, Rs Ag-2; Picolit W-Sw. Rs Ag-2; Pignolo R-Dr, Rs Ag-2; Ribolla Gialla W-Dr, Rs Ag-2

Collio Goriziano or Collio : Bianco W-Dr, Rs Ag-2; Rosso R-Dr, Rs Ag-3; Cabernet R-Dr, Rs Ag-3; Cabernet Franc R-Dr, Rs Ag-3; Cabernet Sauvignon R-Dr, Rs Ag-3; Chardonnay W-Dr, Rs Ag-2; Malvasia W-Dr, Rs Ag-2; Merlot R-Dr, Rs Ag-3; Müller Thurgau W-Dr, Rs Ag-2; Picolit W-Sw; Pinot Bianco W-Dr, Rs Ag-2; Pinot Grigio W-Dr, Rs Ag-2; Pinot Nero R-Dr, Rs Ag-3; Ribolla Gialla W-Dr, Rs Ag-2; Riesling Italico W-Dr, Rs Ag-2; Riesling W-Dr, Rs Ag-2; Sauvignon W-Dr, Rs Ag-2; Tocai Friulano W-Dr, Rs Ag-2; Traminer Aromatico W-Dr, Rs Ag-2

Friuli Annia : Bianco W-Dr/Fz; Rosato P-Dr/Fz; Rosso R-Dr, Rs Ag-2; Spumante W-Dr-Sp; Cabernet Franc R-Dr, Rs Ag-2; Cabernet Sauvignon R-Dr, Rs Ag-2; Chardonnay W-Dr/Fz; Malvasia W-Dr/Fz; Merlot R-Dr, Rs Ag-2; Pinot Bianco W-Dr/Fz; Pinot Grigio W-Dr/Fz; Refosco del Peduncolo Rosso R-Dr, Rs Ag-2; Sauvignon W-Dr; Tocai Friulano W-Dr; Verduzzo Friulano W-Dr/Sw/Fz

Friuli Aquileia : Bianco W-Dr; Rosato P-Dr/Fz; Rosso R-Dr, Rs Ag-2, also Novello; Cabernet R-Dr, Rs Ag-2, also Novello; Cabernet Franc R-Dr, Rs Ag-2, also Novello; Cabernet Sauvignon R-Dr, Rs Ag-2, also Novello; Chardonnay W-Dr/Fz; Chardonnay Spumante W-Dr-Sp; Malvasia Istriana W-Dr/Fz; Merlot R-Dr, Rs Ag-2, also Novello; Müller Thurgau W-Dr/Fz; Pinot Bianco W-Dr; Pinot Grigio W-Dr; Refosco R-Dr, Rs Ag-2, also Novello; Riesling W-Dr; Sauvignon W-Dr; Tocai Friulano W-Dr; Traminer Aromatico W-Dr; Verduzzo Friulano W-Dr/Sw

Friuli Grave : Bianco W-Dr, Rs Ag-2; Rosato P-Dr/Fz; Rosso R-Dr, Rs Ag-2, also Novello; Spumante W-Dr-Sp; Cabernet R-Dr, Rs Ag-2; Cabernet Franc R-Dr, Rs Ag-2; Cabernet Sauvignon R-Dr, Rs Ag-2; Chardonnay W-Dr/Fz/Sp, Rs Ag-2; Merlot R-Dr, Rs Ag-2; Pinot Bianco W-Dr/Fz/Sp, Rs Ag-2; Pinot Grigio W-Dr, Rs Ag-2; Pinot Nero R-Dr, Rs Ag-2; Refosco dal Peduncolo Rosso R-Dr, Rs Ag-2; Riesling W-Dr, Rs Ag-2; Sauvignon W-Dr, Rs Ag-2; Tocai Friulano W-Dr, Rs Ag-2; Traminer Aromatico W-Dr, Rs Ag-2; Verduzzo Friulano W-Dr/Sw/Sp, Rs Ag-2 (All preceding wines except Rosato and Spumante have a Superiore version requiring lower vine yields and a higher degree of natural alcohol)

Friuli Isonzo : Bianco W-Dr/Fz; Rosato P-

Dr/Fz; Rosso R-Dr/Fz; Rosso Spumante R-Dr-Sp; Vendemmia Tardiva W-Dr/Sw; Cabernet R-Dr; Cabernet Franc R-Dr; Cabernet Sauvignon R-Dr; Chardonnay W-Dr; Franconia R-Dr; Malvasia W-Dr; Merlot R-Dr; Moscato Giallo W-Sw; Moscato Giallo Spumante W-Sw-Sp; Moscato Rosa P-Sw; Moscato Rosa Spumante P-Sw-Sp; Pinot Bianco W-Dr/Sp; Pinot Grigio W-Dr; Pinot Spumante W-Dr-Sp; Refosco del Peduncolo Rosso R-Dr; Riesling W-Dr; Riesling Italico W-Dr; Sauvignon W-Dr; Schioppettino R-Dr; Tocai Friulano W-Dr; Traminer Aromatico W-Dr; Verduzzo Friulano W-Dr/Sw/Sp

Friuli Latisana : Rosato P-Dr/Fz, also Novello; Spumante W-Dr-Sp; Cabernet R-Dr, Rs Ag-2, also Novello; Cabernet Franc R-Dr, Rs Ag-2, also Novello; Cabernet Sauvignon R-Dr, Rs Ag-2, also Novello; Chardonnay W-Dr/Fz; Franconia R-Dr, Rs Ag-2, also Novello; Malvasia Istriana W-Dr/Fz; Merlot R-Dr, Rs Ag-2, also Novello; Pinot Bianco W-Dr/Fz; Pinot Grigio W-Dr; Pinot Nero R-Dr/Fz, Rs Ag-2, also Novello; Refosco dal Peduncolo Rosso R-Dr, Rs Ag-2, also Novello; Riesling Renano W-Dr;

Sauvignon W-Dr; Tocai Friulano W-Dr; Traminer Aromatico W-Dr; Verduzzo Friulano W-Dr/Sw/Fz (All preceding wines except Rosato and Spumante have a Superiore version requiring lower vine yields and a higher degree of natural alcohol)

Lison-Pramaggiore (shared with Veneto) : Cabernet R-Dr/Sp, Rs Ag-3; Cabernet Franc R-Dr/Sp, Rs Ag-3; Cabernet Sauvignon R-Dr/Sp, Rs Ag-3; Chardonnay W-Dr/Sp; Refosco del Peduncolo Rosso R-Dr/Sp; Merlot R-Dr/Sp, Rs Ag-2; Pinot Bianco W-Dr/Sp; Pinot Grigio W-Dr/Sp; Riesling Italico W-Dr/Sp; Sauvignon W-Dr/Sp; Tocai Italico W-Dr/Sp; Verduzzo W-Dr/Sw/Sp

IGT (3)

Alto Livenza
Venezia Giulia
Venezie or delle Venezie

Trentino-Alto Adige

Trentino-Alto Adige, Italy's northernmost region, is walled in by the Rhaetian Alps and the Dolomites, so that only about 15 percent of the region's land is cultivable and much that is produces fruit and wine grapes. The difficulty of growing vines on steep, often terraced hillsides compels growers to emphasize quality. About three-quarters of production is DOC and a major share of the wine is exported.

Trentino-Alto Adige, with borders on Austria and Switzerland, is split into two distinct provinces. Trentino, around the city of Trento (or Trent) to the south, is historically Italian in language and culture. Alto Adige, around the city of Bolzano (or Bozen) to the north, is known as Südtirol to the prominent German-speaking population. The South Tyrol, historically part of Austria, is officially bilingual.

Production of the numerous varietal wines is centered in two large DOC zones: Trentino in the south and Alto Adige or Südtirol, the province's blanket appellation. The Alto Adige DOC takes in wines from distinct zones noted for class: Colli di Bolzano/Bozner Leiten, Meranese di Collina/Meraner, Santa Maddalena/St Magdalener, Terlano/Terlan, Valle d'Isarco/Eisacktal, and Val Venosta/Vinschgau.

Although experts agree that the Alpine climate favors grapes for perfumed white wines, the historical emphasis has been on reds, which account for nearly two-thirds of the region's production.

The dominant vine variety of Alto Adige is Schiava or Vernatsch, source of light, bright reds that flow north prodigiously to German-speaking countries. The most highly regarded of these is St Magdalener or Santa Maddalena, grown on the picturesque slopes overlooking Bolzano. The best known wine is Caldaro or Kalterersee, produced from vines around the pretty lake of that name at the rate of nearly 15 million bottles a year.

The ranks of roseate ruby wines from Schiava extend through the South Tyrol along the Adige river into Trentino and Veneto under the Valdadige or Etschtaler appellation. That applies to red and white wines of popular commercial standards. Other reds show greater class. Alto Adige's native Lagrein and Trentino's Teroldego stand with northern Italy's most distinguished vines, making wines of singular personality.

Lagrein thrives on the gravelly plains along the Adige at Gries, a quarter of Bolzano where the wine achieves full, round, plush qualities with a bit of age. Santa Maddalena has a long-standing reputation as a refined light red. Teroldego, grown on the Rotaliano plain north of Trento, is an unusually

Trento (Trent) is the administrative center of Trentino-Alto Adige, whose other province is Bolzano (Bozen). The region ranks 11th in size (13,607 square kilometers) and 16th in population (930,000).

Vineyards cover 13,670 hectares, of which registered DOC plots total 12,900 hectares.

Average annual wine production of 1,200,000 hectoliters (12th) includes about 70% DOC, of which about 60% is red.

attractive red when young, with capacity to age splendidly from good vintages. Trentino's Marzemino makes a fresh, lively red for casual sipping.

In both provinces, increasing space has been devoted to Cabernet Sauvignon and Merlot, which can reach impressive heights whether alone or in blends. The region also produces

some of Italy's finest rosés, the most impressive being Lagrein Kretzer. The sweet Moscato Rosa, with its gracefully flowery aroma, is a rare and prized dessert wine.

The growing demand for white wines has influenced growers to plant more of the international premium varieties. The heights are favorable to aromatic whites: Sylvaner, Veltliner, Gewürztraminer, Müller Thurgau and white Moscato. But the quality of Chardonnay, Pinot Bianco and Grigio and Sauvignon from certain cellars can also stand with Italy's finest. Trentino's native Nosiola makes a a tasty dry white and is also the base of Vino Santo, an opulent dessert wine from the Valle dei Laghi north of Lake Garda.

Although the region's white wines are sometimes considered light by international standards, the best of them have an unexpected propensity to age. Pinot Bianco, Riesling, Sylvaner and Müller Thurgau have been known to remain fresh and vital for a decade or more. But the emphasis remains on the popular Pinot Grigio and, increasingly, on Chardonnay and Gewürztraminer.

Trentino, which boasts Italy's largest production of Chardonnay, is a leader with sparkling wines by the classical method, many of which qualify under the prestigious Trento DOC. Alto Adige has also stepped up sparkling wine production.

Ultimately, producers in both provinces have been making whites of greater weight and complexity—in particular from Chardonnay, Sauvignon, Pinot Bianco and Gewürztraminer, whose name derives from the South Tyrolean village of Tramin.

Red wines have also taken on greater dimensions, notably in Lagrein and Teroldego and combinations of Cabernet and Merlot, but also with Pinot Nero. They are gradually enhancing the status of a region whose sterling record with DOC still hasn't fully expressed the extraordinary quality potential.

Despite the traditional flow north to German-speaking countries, the wines of Trentino-Alto Adige—whites in particular—have been making steady progress in Italy and, recently, on distant markets, such as the United States and United Kingdom.

DOC (7)

Alto Adige/Südtirol/Sudtirolo (Colli di Bolzano/Bozner Leiten, Meranese di Collina/ Meraner, Santa Maddalena/St Magdalener, Terlano/Terlan, Valle d'Isarco/Eisacktal, Val Venosta/Vinschgau) : Bianco/Weiss W-Dr; Bianco/Weiss Passito W-Sw, Rs Ag-2; Spumante W-Dr-Sp, Metodo Classico Ag-1.7, Rs Ag-3; Spumante Rosé or Rosato/Kretzer P-Dr-Sp, Metodo Classico Ag-1.7, Rs Ag-3; Cabernet R-Dr, Rs Ag-2; Cabernet-Lagrein R-Dr, Rs Ag-2; Cabernet-Merlot R-Dr, Rs Ag-2; Cabernet Sauvignon and/or Franc R-Dr, Rs Ag-2, also VT R-Sw; Chardonnay W-Dr, also Passito and VT W-Sw; Chardonnay Spumante W-Dr-Sp, Metodo Classico Ag-1.7, Rs Ag-3; Lagrein Dunkel/Scuro R-Dr, also Gries or Grieser Lagrein, Rs Ag-2, also VT R-Sw; Lagrein Kretzer/Rosato P-Dr, also Gries or Grieser Lagrein; Malvasia/Malvasier R-Dr, also VT R-Sw; Merlot R-Dr, Rs Ag-2, also VT R-Sw; Merlot Rosato/Kretzer P-Dr; Moscato Giallo/Goldenmuskateller W-Dr/Sw, also Passito and VT W-Sw; Moscato Rosa/Rosenmuskateller R-P-Sw, also VT R-P-Sw; Müller Thurgau W-Dr; Pinot Bianco/ Weissburgunder W-Dr/Sp, also Passito and VT W-Sw; Pinot Grigio/Ruländer W-Dr, also

Trentino-Alto Adige

DOC

1 Alto Adige/Südtirol/Sudtirolo*
A Colli di Bolzano/Bozner Leiten
B Meranese di Collina/Meraner
C Santa Maddalena/St Magdalener
D Terlano/Terlan
E Valle d'Isarco/Eisacktal
F Val Venosta/Vinschgau

2 Caldaro or Lago di Caldaro/Kalterersee or Kalterer (Classico/Klassisch)
3 Casteller
4 Teroldego Rotaliano
5 Trentino**
6 Trento**
7 Valdadige/Etschtaler

*Wines may be produced throughout Alto Adige

**Wines may be produced throughout Trentino

Passito and VT W-Sw; Pinot Nero/Blauburgunder R-Dr, Rs Ag-2; Pinot Nero Rosato or Rosé/Blauburgunder Kretzer P-Dr, also VT P-Sw; Pinot Nero/Blauburgunder Spumante W-Dr-Sp or P-Dr-Sp, Metodo Classico Ag-1.7, Rs Ag-3; Riesling Italico/ Welschriesling W-Dr, also VT W-Sw; Riesling Renano/Rheinriesling W-Dr, also Passito and VT W-Sw; Sauvignon W-Dr, also Passito and VT W-Sw; Schiava/Vernatsch R-Dr, also VT R-Sw; Schiava Grigia/Grauvernatsch R-Dr, also VT R-Sw; Sylvaner or Silvaner W-Dr, also Passito and VT W-Sw; Traminer Aromatico/Gewürztraminer W-Dr, also VT W-Sw; **Colli di Bolzano/Bozner Leiten** R-Dr; **Meranese di Collina/Meraner or** **Meraner Hügel** R-Dr (Burgravio or Burggräfler from a special subzone); **Santa Maddalena/St Magdalener** R-Dr (Classico or Klassisch or Klassisches Ursprungsgebiet may apply to wines from the original zone); **Terlano/Terlan** W-Dr/Sp, also Passito and VT W-Sw; Chardonnay W-Dr/Sp, also Passito and VT W-Sw; MüllerThurgau W-Dr/Sp, also Passito and VT W-Sw; Pinot Bianco/Weissburgunder W-Dr/Sp, also Passito and VT W-Sw; Riesling Italico/Weischriesling W-Dr/Sp, also VT W-Sw; Riesling Renano/Rheinriesling W-Dr/Sp, also Passito and VT W-Sw; Sauvignon W-Dr/Sp, also Passito and VT W-Sw; Sylvaner or Silvaner W-Dr/Sp, also Passito and VT W-Sw (Classico or Klassisch or Klassisches

also Scelto or Auslese (Classico or Klassisch may apply to wines from the original zone)

Casteller : R-Dr/Sw, also Sup

Teroldego Rotaliano : R-Dr, also Sup, Rs Ag-2; Rosato P-Dr, also Sup

Trentino (Sorni) : Bianco W-Dr, Rs Ag-2; Rosato or Kretzer P-Dr; Rosso R-Dr, Rs Ag-2; Cabernet R-Dr, Rs Ag-2; Cabernet Franc R-Dr, Rs Ag-2; Cabernet Sauvignon R-Dr, Rs Ag-2; Chardonnay W-Dr, Rs Ag-2; Lagrein R-Dr, Rs Ag-2; Lagrein Rosato P-Dr; Marzemino R-Dr, Rs Ag-2; Merlot R-Dr, Rs Ag-2; Moscato Giallo W-Sw, also Liquoroso W-Sw-Ft; Moscato Rosa P-Sw, also Liquoroso P-Sw-Ft; Müller Thurgau W-Dr; Nosiola W-Dr; Pinot Bianco W-Dr, Rs Ag-2; Pinot Grigio W-Dr; Pinot Nero R-Dr, Rs Ag-2; Rebo R-Dr; Riesling W-Dr; Riesling Italico W-Dr; Sauvignon W-Dr, Rs Ag-2; Traminer Aromatico W-Dr; Vino Santo W-Sw Ag-3
Sorni: Bianco R-Dr; Rosso R-Dr (Vendemmia Tardiva [late harvest] versions are permitted for Chardonnay, Moscato Giallo, Moscato Rosa, Müller Thurgau, Nosiola, Pinot Bianco, Pinot Grigio, Riesling Italico, Riesling Renano, Sauvignon and Traminer Aromatico for richly dry to sweet wines aged for at least 14 months)

Trento : W-Dr-Sp or P-Dr-Sp Ag-1.5, con annata (vintage dated) Ag-2, Rs Ag-3

Valdadige/Etschtaler : Bianco W-Dr; Rosato P-Dr; Rosso R-Dr; Chardonnay W-Dr; Pinot Grigio W-Dr; Pinot Bianco W-Dr; Schiava R-Dr

IGT (4)

**Mitterberg or Mitterberg tra Cauria e Tel or Mitterberg zwischen Gfrill und Töll
Vallagarina
Venezie or delle Venezie
Vigneti delle Dolomiti**

Ursprungsgebiet may apply to wines from the original zone); **Valle Isarco/Eisacktaler** Kerner W-Dr, also Passito and VT W-Sw; Klausner Leitacher R-Dr; MüllerThurgau W-Dr, also Passito and VT W-Sw; Pinot Grigio/Ruländer W-Dr, also Passito and VT W-Sw; Sylvaner or Silvaner W-Dr, also Passito and VT W-Sw; Traminer Aromatico/Gewürztraminer W-Dr, also Passito and VT W-Sw; Veltliner W-Dr, also Passito and VT W-Sw (Bressanone or Brixen or Brixner may apply to wines from the original zone); Val **Venosta/Vinschgau** Chardonnay W-Dr, also Passito and VT W-Sw; Kerner W-Dr, also Passito and VT W-Sw; MüllerThurgau W-Dr, also Passito and VT W-Sw; Pinot Bianco/Weissburgunder W-Dr, also Passito and VT W-Sw; Pinot Grigio/Rüländer W-Dr, also Passito and VT W-Sw; Pinot Nero/Blauburguncer R-Dr, also VT R-Sw; Riesling W-Dr, also Passito and VT W-Sw; Schiava/Vernatsch R-Dr, also VT W-Sw; Traminer Aromatico/Gewürztraminer W-Dr, also Passito and VT W-Sw
(VT in this listing stands for Vendemmia Tardiva for wines from late harvested grapes)

Caldaro or Lago di Caldaro/Kalterersee or Kalterer (Classico/Klassisch) : R-Dr,

Italian Food and Wine

"The main thing to remember about Italian cuisine," says a Florentine chef introducing his cooking courses for foreigners, "is that it doesn't exist. First, because the term cuisine is French, but more important because in my country, thank heaven, we have no uniform way of cooking."

He might have added that "Northern Italian cuisine" was invented abroad, apparently to indicate restaurants that do not serve pizza or spaghetti and meatballs smothered in tomato sauce. To suggest anything more than arbitrary links between the regional dishes of northern Italy—the braised beef and creamy risottos of Piedmont, the seafood and herb-inspired touches of Liguria, the pasta and pork delicacies of Emilia or the schnitzel and dumpling fare of Alto Adige, for instance—is little short of heresy. The same could be said of the southern regions where, however, the flavors of the Mediterranean remain generally more intact than elsewhere.

On analysis, la cucina italiana is a miscellany of regional, provincial, local and family dishes that vary from season to season and cook to cook. It is a deliciously random fund of little treasures, of recipes rarely written down but passed intuitively from one generation to another, modified according to the produce available and enhanced by knowing hands.

What sets the cooking of Italy apart from that of any other country is the variety of ingredients and spontaneity of the preparation. In places you can find the Mediterranean diet at its purest in extra virgin olive oil with durum wheat pasta, bread, fresh herbs, vegetables and fruit, fish and cheese, and wine from the nearest hillside. But you can also find some of the richest fare of Europe with fresh egg pasta and sauces based on butter and cream, meat pâtés and cold cuts, beef, pork, poultry and game, lush pastries and sweets, and wine lists that carry grand old vintages from regions north and south. It depends on the time and place, of course, but wherever you dine in Italy expect to be surprised.

Still, there is no denying that some cooks have attempted to standardize the fare. You can find spaghetti alla carbonara on menus in Milan and costoletta alla milanese in Rome, peperonata in Verona and polenta in Palermo. All healthy citizens regularly eat pasta in some form or other and nearly every village north and south has a pizzeria. But the variations from place to place are infinite, and as any experienced gastronome will insist, you have to travel to the place of origin to taste the foods and wines of Italy together at their authentic best.

Cognoscenti will tell you that the ultimate in fonduta con tartufi (cheese fondue with white truffles) is made around Alba in

Piedmont and served with a local Dolcetto. Sicily's rare pasta con le sarde (with sardines and wild fennel) is at its best around Messina matched with a white from Etna. For zampone sausage with lentils it's Modena and a dry Lambrusco di Sorbara; for risi e bisi (rice and peas) it's Venice and a Tocai from Friuli; for trenette noodles with pesto it's Genoa and a rare white Lumassina; for ossobuco (braised veal shank) and risotto milanese it's Milan and a Barbera from Oltrepò Pavese; for tagliatelle noodles and meat ragù it's Bologna and a hearty red Sangiovese di Romagna; for bistecca alla fiorentina with white beans it's Florence and a robust Chianti Classico. And, of course, for pizza napoletana it's Naples and a vivacious white Asprinio from Aversa.

A typical Italian meal may range through three to five dishes, sometimes more. But let's consider the fundamental courses of antipasti (appetizers or openers), primo (pasta, risotto or soup) and secondo (main courses, usually meat, poultry or fish) with some further suggestions for vegetables, cheeses, fruit and desserts. Here are some matches of foods and wines that complement each other. Still, despite what you might have heard about obligatory pairing of local dishes with local wines, the food of Italy is usually admirably adaptable. So, naturally enough, are the wines. Experiments with other combinations are only to be encouraged.

Antipasti	Wines
Asparagi al burro e parmigiano (asparagus with butter and grated Parmigiano)	Collio Sauvignon
Bagna caôda (raw vegetables dipped into "hot bath" of olive oil, garlic, anchovies)	Barbera d'Asti
Bresaola (sliced air-dried beef of Valtellina)	Valtellina
Carpaccio (paper-thin slices of raw veal with shavings of mushrooms and Grana Padano)	Colli Euganei Merlot
Crostini di fegato (chicken liver pâté on crisp bread)	Chianti Colli Fiorentini
Fiori di zucchini fritti (fried zucchini flowers)	Orvieto Classico
Frutti di mare (raw or poached seafood salad)	Verdicchio dei Castelli di Jesi Classico
Granseola alla veneziana (spider crab minced with olive oil, pepper, lemon and served in its shell)	Soave Classico Superiore
Mozzarella in carrozza (breaded and fried sandwich of buffalo mozzarella and anchovy	Greco di Tufo
Ostriche (raw oysters)	Gavi
Peperonata (stewed peppers)	Cerasuolo di Vittoria
Prosciutto di San Daniele con fichi (Friulian cured raw ham with figs)	Colli Oriental del Friuli Tocai Friulano

Secondi ▨▨▨▨▨▨▨ # Wines ▨▨▨▨

Abbacchio alla cacciatora (baby lamb cooked with rosemary, garlic, anchovies)

Cerveteri Rosso

Arista di maiale (pork loin roast with rosemary, garlic, wild fennel pollen)

Vino Nobile di Montepulciano

Baccalà alla vicentina (dried cod cooked with milk, onions, anchovies, Parmigiano)

Colli Berici Tocai Rosso

Brasato al Barolo (beef braised in Barolo)

Barolo

Bollito misto (beef, veal, hen and sausage simmered and served with sauces such as piquant green salsa verde)

Colli Piacentini Gutturnio

Branzino al forno (baked sea bass)

Collio Bianco Riserva

Fegato alla veneziana (calf's liver sautéed with onions)

Breganze Cabernet

Fritto misto di pesce (crisp fried shrimp, squid and other fresh fish)

Trentino Sauvignon

Melanzane alla parmigiana (eggplant baked with tomato, buffalo mozzarella, Parmigiano)

Vesuvio Rosato

Pollo alla diavola (spicy charcoal grilled chicken)

Rosso Conero

Porceddu (suckling pig roasted on a spit at an open hearth)

Cannonau di Sardegna Secco

Scampi alla griglia (charcoal grilled scampi with lemon and herbs)

Friuli Isonzo Sauvignon

Trota al burro (Alpine brook trout pan roasted with butter and herbs)

Alto Adige Müller Thurgau

Vitello tonnato (cold veal slices with creamy tuna sauce and capers)

Franciacorta Brut Millesimato

Primi

Wines

Bucatini all'amatriciana (slim pasta pipes
with salt pork, chili pepper, sometimes
tomato, grated Pecorino Romano)

Montepulciano d'Abruzzo

Cassòla (spicy Sardinian fish soup with
a dozen types of crustaceans and mollusks)

Vermentino di Gallura

Crespelle con ricotta e spinaci (crêpes rolled and
stuffed with ricotta and spinach)

Alto Adige or Trentino Chardonnay

Fettuccine al burro (egg noodles with butter,
cream, grated Parmigiano)

Frascati Superiore

Gnocchi di patate con ragù (potato gnocchi with
meat sauce and grated cheese)

Valpolicella Classico Superiore

Lasagne al forno (sheets of pasta layered with meat
and bechamel and baked in the oven)

Rosso Piceno

Orecchiette con cime di rapa (ear-shaped pasta with
turnip greens, garlic, chili pepper)

Castel del Monte Rosato

Panissa (thick Piedmontese risotto with
red beans, pork)

Monferrato Barbera

Pasta e fagioli (thick bean soup with pasta)

Friuli Grave Merlot

Ribollita (Tuscan vegetable-bean soup thickened with
bread and topped with extra virgin olive oil)

Morellino di Scansano

Risotto alla certosina (rice with crayfish, frogs, perch,
vegetables and mushrooms)

Oltrepò Pavese Pinot Bianco

Tortelli di zucca (egg pasta envelopes filled with
pumpkin and topped with grated Grana Padano)

Lugana Superiore

Tortellini in brodo (stuffed egg pasta rolls in capon
broth with grated Parmigiano)

Albana di Romagna Secco

Spaghetti alla carbonara (with salt pork, eggs, pepper
and grated Parmigiano and Pecorino Romano)

Velletri Rosso

Spaghetti con le vongole veraci
(with tiny clams sautéed with olive oil, garlic, parsley)

Ischia Biancolella

Formaggi ▰▰▰ Wines ▰▰▰

Mild, soft cheese, such as Bel Paese, Stracchino, Mozzarella di Bufala, Fior di Latte or Ricotta	Light to medium-bodied whites, such as Orvieto, Frascati, Soave, Lugana, Albana di Romagna, Alcamo Bianco, Ischia Bianco, Sauvignon, Verdicchio
Lightly ripened or seasoned cheeses such as Fontina, fresh Pecorino or Caciotta, Toma or Tuma, Robiola, lightly smoked Provola, Burrata	Rosés or light reds, such as Kalterersee, Bardolino, Garda Chiaretto, Dolcetto di Dogliano, Grignolino, Marzemino, Rosato di Salento
Ripe or medium-aged cheeses, such as Grana Padano, Parmigiano Reggiano, Pecorino Toscano, Pecorino Sardo, Asiago, Castelmagno, Monte Veronese, Caciocavallo	Robust, medium-aged reds, such as Barbaresco, Barolo, Barbera d'Asti, Brunello di Montalcino, Torgiano Rosso Taurasi, Aglianico del Vulture, Valtellina Superiore, Alto Adige Lagrein Dunkel, Teroldego Rotaliano
Sharp, very ripe or peppery cheeses, such as Bitto, Provolone Piccante, Gorgonzola Naturale, Pecorino Siciliano, Ragusano, Pecorino Romano	Choices may vary from dry but rich reds, such as Valtellina Sfursat, Amarone della Valpolicella, Montefalco Sagrantino or Primitivo di Manduria to dry fortified wines, such as Marsala Vergine or Vernaccia di Oristano to sweet wines such as Recioto di Soave, Vin Santo, Aleatico or Picolit

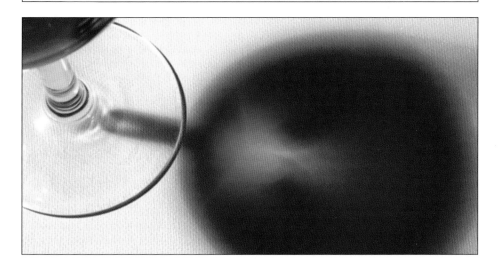

Verdura

The wine to serve with most vegetable dishes or greens depends on whether they are a main course or a side dish. In the second case, the fish, meat or poultry would determine the choice. Most vegetable dishes alone call for a wine on the light side—a white, rosé or young red. Some vegetables, like asparagus and spinach, are hard to match. Others, like raw artichokes or salad with vinegar, are usually better without wine.

Frutta

Italians usually eat fruit fresh and without a specific wine to accompany, though lightly sweet and bubbly Moscato d'Asti or Prosecco or Malvasia go nicely with many things.

Dolci

Desserts can create problems with choices, since Italy has both an astonishing variety of sweets and nearly as many sweet wines, few of them well known abroad. There are some traditional matches: Tuscan almond biscuits with Vin Santo, zabaglione with Marsala Superiore Dolce and Milan's panettone Christmas cake with sparkling Asti. As a rule, lightly sweet desserts go best with lightly sweet wines, so fruit tarts, pound cakes, sherbets and pastries might be matched with gently bubbly Moscato d'Asti or Verduzzo Friulano or a Malvasia from Colli Piacentini or Sardinia. Richer sweets take sweeter or stronger wines, such as Malvasia delle Lipari or Moscato Passito di Pantelleria. It is never easy to find the perfect wine with sweets laced with chocolate, rum, candied fruit or spices, such as ginger or cinnamon, though that doesn't stop gourmets from trying.

Index of DOC and DOCG Wines

DOCG

A

Acqui or Brachetto d'Acqui, Piedmont, 70
Albana di Romagna, Emilia-Romagna, 60
Asti, Piedmont, 70

B

Barbaresco, Piedmont, 70
Bardolino Superiore, Veneto, 79
Barolo, Piedmont, 70
Brunello di Montalcino, Tuscany, 52

C

Carmignano, Tuscany, 52
Chianti, Tuscany, 52
Chianti Classico, Tuscany, 52

F

Franciacorta, Lombardy, 66

G

Gattinara, Piedmont, 70
Gavi or Cortese di Gavi, Piedmont, 70
Ghemme, Piedmont, 70

M

Montefalco Sagrantino,Umbria, 49

R

Recioto di Soave, Veneto, 79

T

Taurasi, Campania, 34
Torgiano Rosso Riserva, Umbria, 49

V

Valtellina Superiore, Lombardy, 66
Vermentino di Gallura, Sardinia, 23
Vernaccia di San Gimignano, Tuscany, 52
Vino Nobile di Montepulciano, Tuscany, 52

DOC

A

Aglianico del Taburno, Campania, 34
Aglianico del Vulture, Basilicata 29
Albugnano, Piedmont, 70
Alcamo or Bianco d'Alcamo, Sicily, 19
Aleatico di Gradoli, Apulia, 31
Aleatico di Puglia, Apulia, 31
Alezio, Apulia, 31
Alghero, Sardinia, 23
Alto Adige, Trentino-Alto Adige, 87
Ansonica Costa dell'Argentario, Tuscany, 52
Aprilia, Latium, 39
Arborea, Sardinia, 23
Arcole, Veneto, 79
Assisi, Umbria, 49
Atina, Latium, 39
Aversa, Campania, 34

B

Bagnoli di Sopra or Bagnoli, Veneto, 79
Barbera d'Alba, Piedmont, 70
Barbera d'Asti, Piedmont, 70
Barco Reale di Carmignano, Tuscany, 52
Barbera del Monferrato, Piedmont, 70
Bardolino, Veneto, 79
Bianchello del Metauro, Marches, 46
Bianco Capena, Latium, 39

Bianco della Valdinievole, Tuscany, 52
Bianco dell'Empolese, Tuscany, 52
Bianco di Custoza, Veneto, 79
Bianco di Pitigliano, Tuscany, 52
Bianco Pisano di San Torpé, Tuscany, 52
Biferno, Molise, 42
Bivongi, Calabria, 26
Boca, Piedmont, 70
Bolgheri and Bolgheri Sassicaia, Tuscany, 52
Bosco Eliceo, Emilia-Romagna, 60
Botticino, Lombardy, 66
Bramaterra, Piedmont, 70
Breganze, Veneto, 79
Brindisi, Apulia, 39

C

Cacc'e mmitte di Lucera, Apulia, 31
Cagnina di Romagna, Emilia-Romagna, 60
Caldaro or Lago di Caldano, Trentino-Alto
    Adige, 87
Campi Flegrei, Campania, 34
Campidano di Terralba or Terralba, Sardinia, 23
Canavese, Piedmont, 70
Candia dei Colli Apuani, Tuscany, 52
Cannonau di Sardegna, Sardinia, 23
Capalbio, Tuscany, 52
Capri, Campania, 34
Capriano del Colle, Lombardy, 66
Carema, Piedmont, 70
Carignano del Sulcis, Sardinia, 23
Carmignano, Tuscany, 52
Carso, Friuli-Venezia Giulia, 83
Castel del Monte, Apulia, 31
Castel San Lorenzo, Campania, 34
Casteller, Trentino-Alto Adige, 87
Castelli Romani, Latium, 39
Cellatica, Lombardy, 66
Cerasuolo di Vittoria, Sicily, 19
Cerveteri, Latium, 39

Cesanese del Piglio, Latium, 39
Cesanese di Affile, Latium, 39
Cesanese di Olevano Romano, Latium, 39
Cilento, Campania, 34
Cinque Terre and Cinque Terre Sciacchetrà,
    Liguria, 64
Cirò, Calabria, 26
Colli Albani, Latium, 39
Colli Altotiberini, Umbria, 49
Colli Amerini, Umbria, 49
Colli Berici, Veneto, 79
Colli Bolognesi, Emilia-Romagna, 60
Colli Bolognesi Classico Pignoletto, Emilia-
    Romagna, 60
Colli del Trasimeno, Umbria, 49
Colli della Sabina, Latium, 39
Colli dell'Etruria Centrale, Tuscany, 52
Colli di Conegliano, Veneto, 79
Colli di Faenza, Emilia-Romagna, 60
Colli di Luni, Tuscany, Liguria, 54/64
Colli di Parma, Emilia-Romagna, 60
Colli di Rimini , Emilia-Romagna, 60
Colli di Scandiano e Canossa, Emilia-
    Romagna, 60
Colli d'Imola, Emilia-Romagna, 60
Colli Etruschi Viterbesi, Latium, 39
Colli Euganei, Veneto, 79
Colli Lanuvini, Latium, 39
Colli Maceratesi, Marches, 46
Colli Martani, Umbria, 49
Colli Orientali del Friuli, Friuli-Venezia Giulia, 83
Colli Perugini, Umbria, 49
Colli Pesaresi, Marches, 46
Colli Piacentini, Emilia-Romagna, 60
Colli Tortonesi, Piedmont, 70
Collina Torinese, Piedmont, 70
Colline di Levanto, Liguria, 64
Colline Lucchesi, Tuscany, 52
Colline Novaresi, Piedmont, 70
Colline Saluzzesi, Piedmont, 70

Collio Goriziano or Collio, Friuli-Venezia
   Giulia, 83
Contea di Sclafani, Campania, 34
Contessa Entellina, Sicily, 19
Controguerra, Abruzzi, 44
Copertino, Apulia, 31
Cori, Latium, 39
Cortese dell'Alto Monferrato, Piedmont, 70
Cortona, Tuscany, 52
Costa d'Amalfi, Campania, 34
Coste della Sesia, Piedmont, 70

D

Delia Nivolelli, Sicily, 19
Dolcetto d'Acqui, Piedmont, 70
Dolcetto d'Alba, Piedmont, 70
Dolcetto d'Asti, Piedmont, 70
Dolcetto delle Langhe Monregalesi,
   Piedmont, 70
Dolcetto di Diano d'Alba, Piedmont, 70
Dolcetto di Dogliani, Piedmont, 70
Dolcetto di Ovada,Piedmont, 70
Donnici, Calabria, 26

E

Elba, Tuscany, 52
Eloro, Sicily, 19
Erbaluce di Caluso or Caluso, Piedmont, 70
Esino, Marches, 46
Est! Est!! Est!!! di Montefiascone, Latium, 39
Etna, Sicily, 19

F

Falerio dei Colli Ascolani or Falerio, Marches, 46
Falerno del Massico, Campania, 34
Fara, Piedmont, 70
Faro, Sicily, 19
Fiano di Avellino, Campania, 34
Frascati, Latium, 39
Freisa d'Asti, Piedmont, 70

Freisa di Chieri, Piedmont, 70
Friuli Annia, Friuli-Venezia Giulia, 83
Friuli Aquileia, Friuli-Venezia Giulia, 83
Friuli Grave, Friuli-Venezia Giulia, 83
Friuli Isonzo, Friuli-Venezia Giulia, 83
Friuli Latisana, Friuli-Venezia Giulia, 84

G

Gabiano, Piedmont, 70
Galatina, Apulia, 31
Galluccio, Campania, 34
Gambellara, Veneto, 79
Garda, Lombardy & Veneto, 66/79
Garda Colli Mantovani, Lombardy, 66
Genazzano, Latium, 39
Gioia del Colle, Apulia, 31
Girò di Cagliari, Sardinia, 23
Golfo del Tigullio, Liguria, 64
Gravina, Apulia, 31
Greco di Bianco, Calabria, 26
Greco di Tufo, Campania, 34
Grignolino d'Asti, Piedmont, 70
Grignolino del Monferrato Casalese,
   Piedmont, 70
Guardia Sanframondi or Guardiolo,
   Campania, 34

I

Ischia, Campania, 34

L

Lacrima di Morro d'Alba, Marches, 46
Lago di Corbara, Umbria, 49
Lambrusco di Sorbara, Emilia-Romagna, 60
Lambrusco Grasparossa di Castelvetro,
   Emilia-Romagna, 60
Lambrusco Mantovano, Lombardy, 66
Lambrusco Salamino di Santa Croce,
   Emilia-Romagna, 60
Lamezia, Calabria, 26

Langhe, Piedmont, 70
Lessini Durello, Veneto, 79
Lessona, Piedmont, 70
Leverano, Apulia, 31
Lison-Pramaggiore, Veneto, Friuli-Venezia
 Giulia, 79/83
Lizzano, Apulia, 31
Loazzolo, Piedmont, 70
Locorotondo, Apulia, 31
Lugana, Lombardy, Veneto, 66/79

Malvasia delle Lipari, Sicily, 19
Malvasia di Bosa, Sardinia, 23
Malvasia di Cagliari, Sardinia, 23
Malvasia di Casorzo d'Asti, Piedmont, 70
Malvasia di Castelnuovo Don Bosco,
 Piedmont, 70
Mandrolisai, Sardinia, 23
Marino, Latium, 39
Marsala, Sicily, 19
Martina or Martina Franca, Apulia, 31
Matino, Apulia, 31
Melissa, Calabria, 26
Menfi, Sicily, 19
Molise, Molise, 42
Monferrato, Piedmont, 70
Monica di Cagliari, Sardinia, 23
Monica di Sardegna, Sardinia, 23
Monreale, Sicily, 19
Montecarlo, Tuscany, 52
Montecompatri Colonna, Latium, 39
Montecucco, Tusany, 52
Montefalco, Umbria, 49
Montello e Colli Asolani, Veneto, 79
Montepulciano d'Abruzzo, Abruzzi, 44
Monteregio di Massa Marittima, Tuscany, 52
Montescudaio, Tuscany, 52
Moscadello di Montalcino, Tuscany, 52
Moscato di Cagliari, Sardinia, 23

Moscato di Noto, Sicily, 19
Moscato di Pantelleria, Sicily, 19
Moscato di Sardegna, Sardinia, 23
Moscato di Siracusa, Sicily, 19
Moscato di Sorso Sennori, Sardinia, 23
Moscato di Trani, Apulia, 31
Moscato Passito di Pantelleria, Sicily, 19

Nardò, Apulia, 31
Nasco di Cagliari, Sardinia, 23
Nebbiolo d'Alba, Piedmont, 70
Nuragus di Cagliari, Sardinia, 23

Oltrepò Pavese, Lombardy, 66
Orcia, Tuscany, 52
Orta Nova, Apulia, 31
Orvieto, Umbria, Latium, 39/49
Ostuni, Apulia, 31

Pagadebit di Romagna, Emila-Romagna, 60
Parrina,Tuscany, 52
Penisola Sorrentina, Campania, 34
Pentro di Isernia or Pentro, Molise, 42
Piemonte, Piedmont, 70
Pinerolese, Piedmont, 70
Pollino, Calabria, 26
Pomino, Tuscany, 52
Primitivo di Manduria, Apulia, 31
Prosecco di Conegliano-Valdobbiadene,
 Veneto, 79

R

Reggiano, Emilia-Romagna, 60
Reno, Emilia-Romagna, 60
Riviera del Garda Bresciano, Lombardy, 66
Riviera Ligure di Ponente, Liguria, 64
Roero, Piedmont, 70

Romagna Albana Spumante,
  Emila-Romagna, 60
Rossese di Dolceacqua or Dolceacqua,
  Liguria, 64
Rosso Barletta, Apulia, 31
Rosso Canosa or Canasium, Apulia, 31
Rosso Conero, Marches, 46
Rosso di Cerignola, Apulia, 31
Rosso di Montalcino, Tuscany, 52
Rosso di Montepulciano, Tuscany, 52
Rosso Orvietano or Orvietano Rosso,
  Umbria, 49
Rosso Piceno, Marches, 46
Rubino di Cantavenna, Piedmont, 70
Ruché di Castagnole Monferrato, Piedmont, 70

S

Salice Salentino, Apulia, 31
Sambuca di Sicilia, Sicily, 19
San Colombano al Lambro, Lombardy, 66
San Gimignano, Tuscany, 52
San Martino della Battaglia, Lombardy,
  Veneto, 66/79
San Severo, Apulia, 31
San Vito di Luzzi, Calabria, 26
Sangiovese di Romagna, Emilia-Romagna, 60
Sannio, Campania, 34
Santa Margherita di Belice, Sicily, 19
Sant'Agata dei Goti, Campania, 34
Sant'Antimo, Tuscany, 52
Sardegna Semidano, Sardinia, 23
Savuto, Calabria, 26
Scavigna, Calabria, 26
Sciacca, Sicily, 19
Sizzano, Piedmont, 70
Soave, Veneto, 79
Solopaca, Campania, 34
Sovana, Tuscany, 52
Squinzano, Apulia, 31

T

Taburno, Campania, 34
Tarquinia, Latium, 39
Teroldego Rotaliano, Trentino-Alto Adige, 87
Terre di Franciacorta, Lombardy, 66
Torgiano, Umbria, 49
Trebbiano d'Abruzzo, Abruzzi, 44
Trebbiano di Romagna, Emilia-Romagna, 60
Trentino, Trentino-Alto Adige, 87
Trento, Trentino-Alto Adige, 87

V

Val d'Arbia, Tuscany, 52
Val di Cornia, Tuscany, 52
Val Polcevera, Liguria, 64
Valcalepio, Lombardy, 66
Valdadige, Veneto & Trentino-Alto Adige, 79/87
Valdichiana, Tuscany, 52
Valle d'Aosta or Vallée d' Aoste, 75
Valpolicella, (Valpantena, Amarone della
  Valpolicella), Veneto, 79
Valsusa, Piedmont, 70
Valtellina, Lombardy, 66
Velletri, Latium, 39
Verbicaro, Calabria, 26
Verdicchio dei Castelli di Jesi, Marches, 46
Verdicchio di Matelica, Marches, 46
Verduno Pelaverga or Verduno, Piedmont, 70
Vermentino di Sardegna, Sardinia, 23
Vernaccia di Oristano, Sardinia, 23
Vernaccia di Serrapetrona, Marches, 46
Vesuvio, Campania, 34
Vignanello, Latium, 39
Vin Santo del Chianti, Tuscany, 52
Vin Santo del Chianti Classico, Tuscany, 52
Vin Santo di Montepulciano, Tuscany, 52
Vini del Piave or Piave, Veneto, 79

Z

Zagarolo, Latium, 39

Other References on Italian Wine

Burton Anderson is the author of Burton Anderson's Best Italian Wines; Wines of Italy (pocket guide); The Wine Atlas of Italy and Traveller's Guide to the Vineyards; Franciacorta, Italy's Sanctuary of Sparkling Wine and Vino, the Wines and Winemakers of Italy.

Other sources recommended by the author for reference or reading include:

- Barolo to Valpolicella, the Wines of Northern Italy, Nicolas Belfrage
- Italian Wines 2001, Gambero Rosso
- Tuscany and its Wines, Hugh Johnson
- The New Italy: A Complete Guide to Contemporary Italian Wine, Marco Sabellico and Daniele Cernilli
- Barolo, Tar and Roses—a Study of the Wines of Alba, Michael Garner and Paul Merritt
- The Story of Wine, Hugh Johnson
- The Oxford Companion to Wine, edited by Jancis Robinson
- Oz Clarke's Wine Guide (at **www.winetoday.com**), Oz Clarke